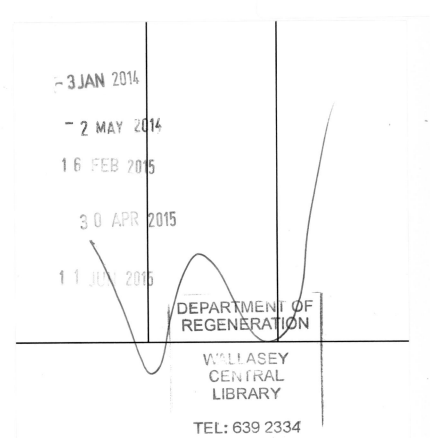

I would like to express my thanks to Ruth Calma who read the original manuscript and gave me so much encouragement.

TO

My husband Nevil
My daughters Lynne and Karen
My son-in-law Steven and
My granddaughters Jennifer Catherine and
Gillian Helen.

First published 1990 by Countyvise Limited, 1 & 3 Grove Road, Rock Ferry, Birkenhead, Wirral, Merseyside L42 3XS.

Copyright © Beryl Wade, 1990.

Photoset and printed by Birkenhead Press Limited, 1 & 3 Grove Road, Rock Ferry, Birkenhead, Merseyside L42 3XS.

ISBN 0 907768 33 4.

Acknowledgements

The author and the publishers would like to thank The Liverpool Central Library, William Brown Street, for their help and co-operation, especially the Micro Film Department where the author spent many hours researching facts and figures, also the Record Office & Local History Department who have granted permission for the reproduction of copyright photographs.

The author and the publishers would also like to thank The Liverpool Daily Post & Echo for allowing the reproduction of factual material from the Liverpool Echo published during the war years.

The author would like to thank the members of the Liverpool Writer's Club and members of Scottie '83 Writer's Workshop for their helpful and constructive criticism of the original manuscript.

The author would also like to thank Mr. Ken Taylor of Liverpool Libraries for his help in obtaining photographs.

CONTENTS

CHAPTER 1.

"The leaving of Liverpool"

1

I was six years old and it was Saturday morning. Just another ordinary Saturday morning, or so I thought as I snuggled down amongst the warm, cosy bedclothes.

My parents owned a sweets, tobacconists and newsagents shop in City Road, Walton, Liverpool and, as I lay comfortably in bed, all the familiar sounds of home wafted around my ears. The tinkle of sweets being weighed on the scales, the noise of traffic in the busy street, the buzz of conversation and the ring of the bell on the door of the shop downstairs. All these were part of my safe and happy world which was all too soon to be torn apart.

I got out of bed and made my way downstairs to the living room.

"Oh good, you're up" said my mother, busily digging for 'change' in the tin cash box which was always kept on the sideboard in our living room. "Wait a minute until I've finished serving and then I'll come and get your breakfast".

A large curtain hung over the doorway that divided our living room from the shop area. I peeped round the curtain and saw that it was full of customers waiting to 'pay their papers' and purchase sweets and cigarettes in readiness for the week-end.

As soon as I had finished eating I joined my parents in the shop helping to serve those customers indulgent enough to allow me to do so. When we had a free moment Mother went in to put the kettle on and make a pot of tea. Whilst she drank she scribbled busily on a piece of paper and counted out some money from her purse.

I always went for the 'messages' on a Saturday morning and thoroughly enjoyed these little excursions for I would meet up with some of my friends and we would stop and chatter just like the grown-ups. With a bit of luck I might even be able to buy some sweets from Jones' the sweetshop over the road.

It might seem odd that I, living in a sweet shop, should want to buy sweets elsewhere but the reasoning behind this was that I wanted to be served like an ordinary customer and in Jones' I would be asked what I wanted and treated like a 'proper customer'. To my mind that was much better than being given a few sweets in a bag by my parents. There was no conflict of business interest in this arrangement as Mr. and Mrs. Jones also had a daughter, Coyla, the same age as myself, and she returned the honours by purchasing sweets in our shop for exactly the same reason.

What sweets we had in those days and how cheap compared to today's prices. Lamb chops, new potatoes and green peas, sweet tobacco, sticky lice, Cadbury's chocolate bars ranging from ½d to 2d for the big unwrapped bars together with a wide variety of loose sweets at 1d and 2d a quarter all awaited the would be young purchasers eager to spend their pocket money.

City Road was always busy on a Saturday morning and would get even more so in the afternoon when the crowds converged on Goodison Park, the home of Everton Football Club or the "School of Science" as my father and other keen Everton supporters called it. Often I would go out amongst these crowds for, in those days, one never feared football crowds. In all the time we lived in City Road, I can never remember any trouble occurring. The mounted police were on duty for the purpose of crowd control but I think their major problem was stopping over-enthusiastic young fans trying to gain free entry by climbing over the fence or obtaining a free view from the roof of St. Luke's Church which was right alongside the football ground.

I collected my list and money and set off just like any other Saturday, only today was no ordinary Saturday. The date was 2nd September, 1939 and before the end of the day my life and that of thousands of others would undergo momentous changes.

As I walked along the road I saw my friend Elsie waving eagerly from the other side. As soon as the road was clear she ran across.

"Have you heard the news? The war's started" she cried excitedly. "It was on the wireless this morning".

"No it hasn't" I contradicted "Mummy and Daddy would have told me".

"If you don't believe me, go and ask your mother" Elsie said.

For a moment I stared at her dumbfounded. Could it be true? No, surely not. We were all aware that the dark clouds of war had been gathering for some time. No matter how hard the adults tried to make light of it, we children knew it was coming. Preparations for the defence of the country had made it blatantly obvious.

We had all been issued with gas masks, just in case. As I was six years old I received a normal mask. The under fives got Mickey Mouse ones, so designed to make the wearing of them less fearful. They were horrible contraptions; they smelt strongly of rubber, bit into the skin under your chin and pulled your hair whenever you put them on or took them off. You couldn't even speak properly in them

7

for your voice took on a muffled, undecipherable tone. Looking at Elsie, I realised she was not joking so, messages forgotten, I ran back home as fast as my legs would carry me.

"Mummy, mummy" I cried, bursting into the shop unceremoniously "the war's started. I just met Elsie and she said it was on the wireless this morning".

Mother grabbed my arm and pulled me quickly into the living room.

"Now listen to me" she said calmly "the war hasn't started yet. Germany has invaded Poland but we're not in it yet".

I usually believed everything my parents told me and trusted them completely but now, for some strange reason, doubts and fears began to fill my mind. Could she just be saying that so I wouldn't be frightened.

I went out again. Elsie had now been joined by some other children and they were all busy discussing the war. Some were even speculating on when the first bombs would be dropped. My stomach knotted with fear. I was sure now that my mother hadn't told me the truth. The war had started, there was no doubt about it. They couldn't all be wrong. Mother was, in fact, quite right. Hostilities between this country and Germany did not commence until the following day, Sunday, 3rd September, 1939.

Some of the children were discussing the possibility of being evacuated to the country and suddenly that was what I wanted. Fear had gripped my mind and my imagination was working overtime. Any minute now we would be attacked, bombs would fall and blow us up, gas attacks would kill us. Oh, the horrors a fertile young mind can dream up within such a short space of time.

Some months earlier, I had stood by the kitchen table watching my mother making pastry and asked "Mummy, what's a war like?". My mother's reply had evidently not satisfied my curiosity for I had gone on to express the wish that "it would be nice if we could have one, just for a few weeks, to see what it was really like". Mother was not enthusiastic about this, nor was my father. Not surprising really, they had already lived through the horrors of the First World War.

Now it was upon us I was not nearly so keen to see what it was really like. I listened to the others discussing the plans for their evacuation and wondered whether I would be able to go away as well. Some of the children were going away with their school and seemed very well informed about the arrangements.

Most of the local children attended either Arnot Street or Gwladys Street, the two big schools in the area, I went to a small school in Spellow Lane. Arrangements had been in hand for some time to evacuate the large Council schools as soon as the authorities felt it was expedient to do so. The children attending these schools had obviously known about the plan for some time.

As that dreadful morning progressed, I eavesdropped unashamedly on as many conversations in the shop as I could. It seemed to me that everyone was talking of war and my fears mounted minute by minute.

"Please, please can I go away too?" I begged.

"Mummy, the bombs might start any minute now, please can I go away?"

What my poor parents thought of all this, I don't know. To have one's own child pleading to be taken away must have been heartrending. I didn't fear for my parents who I would leave behind, I was quite sure they would be safe. Maybe I thought they would be protected because, in my mind, parents were invincible, nothing could ever happen to them. I loved them dearly but could not control the mounting fear and terror inside me.

Strangely enough, never again, not even through all the dreadful horrors of the blitz that was to come later, did I ever experience the same feeling of cold terror as I did that day. Without doubt, that was the worst day of the war for me, albeit that it hadn't even officially begun. What a powerful emotion fear of the unknown is.

After some time and many earnest conversations, it was finally decided that I should go and stay with Aunty Doris and Uncle Harry for a while. Aunty Doris was my father's sister and she and my Uncle had recently moved to Blacon, a little village near Chester. They lived in a delightful bungalow called "Rose Cottage" which was surrounded on one side by fields and on the other by equally pretty bungalows similar to their own. They owned a goodly bit of land, part of which was given over to the producing of vegetables for their own use, part to an orchard which also served as a hen run for about fifty fowl whilst the rest was put over to flowerbeds and a large lawn on which they kept tethered a nanny goat. Along the front of the lawn ran a small stream which flowed into a large pond in the field beyond. It was like going on holiday to go to Aunty Doris' and I couldn't wait to get there.

Mother packed a small bag for me and it was then that we discovered there was very little prospect of getting any public transport that day. Most of it had already been commandeered for evacuation purposes. How were we to get across to Woodside Station?

Mother remembered that one of our customers drove a lorry. She went round to see him and he agreed to take us to Woodside from where we might be able to get a train to Chester. By now things were getting pretty chaotic. It seemed to me that, within the space of a few hours, most of the children were going away, all public transport had virtually come to a standstill save for evacuation purposes and an air of apprehension hung heavily over the City. What a day, the world seemed to have turned upside down.

After dinner, washed, changed and buttoned up in my coat, we were ready to depart. We drove down City Road, Goodison Road, turned into Spellow Lane and then along Walton Road. As we approached the centre of Liverpool what a sight met our eyes. Crowds of children stood together on the pavements, cases by their sides. Some carried brown paper carrier bags or parcels tied up with string and all had a luggage label pinned to their coats or, in the case of the more unfortunate ones who didn't own coats, pinned to their jerseys

Through the Mersey tunnel we travelled, emerging into the light once again at Birkenhead. Turning towards Woodside, we found it jam-packed with more crowds of children all wearing the — by now familiar — luggage labels. Our driver found somewhere to stop and we clambered down.

We were fortunate enough to get on a train stopping at Chester. It was a "special" taking some children to Chester and others further on again into Shrewsbury. As soon as we arrived in Chester we walked the short distance to the Town Hall to catch the bus to Blacon. As we approached, here again, the road was crowded with children; all waiting outside the Town Hall to be billeted. Some of the little ones were crying and older brothers and sisters were comforting and fussing over them. I felt very glad I was going to Aunty Doris' and not to strangers as they were.

An hour or so later we finally arrived at "Rose Cottage" to be greeted by Aunty Doris.

"Oh Nora, I'm so glad you've brought Beryl" she cried "The Billeting Officer has been round to see if we would take a child. Of course we said yes, but oh I was so hoping you'd bring Beryl."

We went indoors and, whilst Aunty Doris made a pot of tea, mother helped me unpack and put my things away in the front bedroom where Aunty said I was to sleep.

As we sat at the table with our cups of tea I began to get fidgety. Grown-up talk I usually found boring and I longed to go out and see the hens, the goat and all the other delights.

"Can I go and see the hens?" I asked.

"Sssh, sssh, there's a good girl. Be quiet now whilst we're talking". No-one was taking any notice. They were all too deeply engrossed in really serious grown-up talk.

After a while, mother said she had "Better get back now". I asked her why she was crying but she just smiled, rubbed the back of her hand across her eyes and told me not to be silly, she wasn't crying, she'd just got something in her eye.

Aunty Doris, Uncle Harry and I stood at the gate and waved to her all the way down the road until she disappeared from sight. What thoughts must have gone through her mind at that time. To have to leave your child and return home not really knowing when you would be together again must have been heartbreaking.

I was lucky, I was with relatives. Some parents had to face sending their children to strangers not knowing who, or where, they were. At that time, the parents suffered more than the children.

A letter home.

Deare Mmmy & dadely
I have been wodering you
have reterned hom
quite saf reelee I do
enjoy feeding the hens
wen you a ent home on
saterdy I went home
qieldy I started give
the hens a feed the hens
are crowing early in the
morning but I am very
happy her I must shut up
now I you dont forget
to send me a letter good.
byou X xxxxxxxxxxxxxxx

CHAPTER 2

"Rose Cottage"

2

Life at Blacon was a complete contrast for me. A City child born and bred, I was used to waking each morning to the sounds of traffic, the low hum of conversation, the occasional shouts as neighbours greeted each other and, of course, the inevitable and all-pervading whistling of delivery boys. This was the pulsating, throbbing City at its best. Plenty of life, plenty of people and a happy noisy bustling air of activity.

At "Rose Cottage" I awoke to the sounds of birds singing, hens clucking and squawking as they milled around the mesh door of the hen run frantically trying to climb over each other in an attempt to get nearest to the spot where my Aunty would enter with their morning mash. Even the air smelt different. In the City, acrid traffic fumes mingling with the wispy smoke from soot blackened chimneys and the salty, muddy smell of the Mersey attacked your nostrils from the first moment of wakefulness. We took it as normal, for it was an integral part of our lives and was even, according to some medical men, the cause of our accent. Here, however, at Blacon, the air was sweet with the smell of grass and trees and the heady fragrance of chickweed which flourished near the hen run. It was also that rare commodity, almost unknown to the City dweller — clean, fresh air.

I soon settled down with Aunty Doris and Uncle Harry and each morning awoke to new experiences. The hens had to be fed and I loved this job. Once the mash was prepared we carried it out to the hen run in a large bucket. The hens would climb over each other and make a fearful noise and it was difficult to get the door open for they would fly on top of the bucket and try to help themselves as we entered. Scooping large handfuls out of the bucket, we filled the troughs and I watched fascinated as they scrabbled and fought to get at the food as though they had never had a meal before.

I loved the hens and there were certainly enough of them. At that time Aunty Doris and Uncle Harry kept about fifty laying hens together with a couple of cockerels. The cockerels were proud and beautiful. They strutted around like peacocks and I longed to be able to pick one up and cuddle it.

One day Aunty Doris caught me trying to do just that. She warned me never to try and pick up the cockerels for they could be quite vicious. Unbeknown to anyone I had, prior to this, been chasing them about quite unmercifully. Neither of the cockerels had ever tried to touch me, not even when I got perilously near to one during

14

an attempt at trying to corner it round the side of the hen run. Instead it had jumped up and down, angrily flapping its wings and squawking its displeasure at the top of its voice. Desperate for a means of escape, it finally shot blindly through my legs as I bent towards it, put on an impressive turn of speed, slid in the mud and finally lost its balance ending up in the ignominious position of beak first against a damson tree.

The hens were a different kettle of fish altogether. Usually slow and lethargic, content to peck aimlessly in the grass they were, however, quite capable of fast bursts of speed when the fancy took them. I was, however, often quite successful in my attempts at hen catching. They felt warm and soft as I carefully lifted them into my arms, their feathers a mixture of softness and prickles as I ran my hand gently down their backs.

One hen in particular, was my favourite. She was a beautiful cream coloured creature and I christened her 'Dorothy'. In the afternoon, when it was time for the hens to have their corn, I singled Dorothy out for special treatment. She was my pet. Soon, even Aunty Doris and Uncle Harry were referring to her as 'Dorothy'. Years later, Aunty Doris confessed to me that Dorothy had eventually died of old age. Apparently neither she nor Uncle Harry had ever been able to bring themselves to 'kill her off'. Dorothy must have been the only hen to have been kept and fed after her useful egg producing life was over.

Each evening the hens would be shut up for the night in the hen house. Much to the amusement of my Aunt and Uncle, I took upon myself the job of 'singing the hens to sleep'. There I stood, warbling lullabies to about fifty hens shut up in the hen house whilst Aunty Doris and Uncle Harry, helpless with mirth, watched surreptitiously from their vantage point at the kitchen window.

Of course, the hard facts of poultry keeping had never entered my head. I fondly believed they were kept purely and simply as pets and for the eggs they produced. However, one Saturday evening, as I was happily playing in the living room, I heard Uncle Harry come into the kitchen.

"I'll go and kill the fowl off for you now" I heard him say.

I couldn't believe my ears. Rushing into the kitchen I cried "Uncle Harry isn't going to kill one of the hens is he?"

"It's alright love, it's only the old one that's finished laying" replied Aunty Doris "We'll have it for dinner tomorrow."

15

It was most certainly not alright. I begged, pleaded, cried. All to no avail. Aunty Doris couldn't understand what was the matter with me. I was inconsolable and wept buckets. Even more so when Uncle Harry later appeared in the kitchen with the 'body' still in its feathers. He, of course, had been blissfully unaware of my reaction to his previous seemingly innocent remark.

"What's up with her?" he asked, nodding at me. The now very dead hen dangled from his hand. I took one look and buried my head in Aunty Doris' skirts and howled anew.

"She's upset about the hen" explained Aunty Doris, reaching for a towel with which to mop my eyes.

Uncle Harry, ignoring what he obviously thought was a big fuss about nothing, put the hen on the draining board in readiness for plucking. It's legs dangled limply over the side.

Aunty Doris drew my head away from her skirts.

"Come on love, don't cry there's a good girl" she soothed. I spotted the legs and was off again.

"For goodness sake Harry, don't leave it there. Shove it in the shed or something" exploded Aunty Doris exasperatedly.

Uncle Harry picked up the offending corpse and quickly disappeared.

Needless to say, I did not have very much appetite for dinner the following day and, strangely enough, neither did Aunty Doris.

In the months that followed, chicken appeared on the menu several times. Whenever I enquired about the source of this largesse I was quickly told it had been bought from Chester market. I accepted this and happily ate my share; I was used to seeing chickens for sale in the shops but never, never, never, did I equate them with the noisy, boisterous hens that pecked so happily in the grass at the back of the cottage. Aunty Doris and Uncle Harry must have kept all their dark and deadly deeds well hidden from me after that unfortunate episode. Oh what a happy, innocent life we City children led.

I soon made friends with the local children. Aunty Doris was very friendly with Mrs. Ellis who lived in one of the cottages further up the lane. Mrs. Ellis had a daughter, Sheila, who was about the same age as myself and we soon became firm friends. Sheila and her older brother, introduced me to some of their friends and they generously included me in all their games.

One day, the boys decided that it was essential to build an air-raid shelter. They drew up their plans and made much play of choosing a suitable site. Sheila and I tagged on behind. We were not included in these vital deliberations being mere girls. As soon as the ideal site had been chosen and the serious business of digging began Sheila and I were suddenly popular again. We could help with the digging!

After a couple of days getting muddy and dirty and making no noticeable progress, Sheila and I judiciously withdrew our services. Our departure was hailed with much scoffing and smug grins from the boys but we just ignored them and went about our own business. We'd had enough. They'd never finish it we told them but they argued hotly that they most certainly would. "Just you wait and see" they chorused.

We waited. A few days later, sitting in the long grass, Sheila suddenly nudged me. "Look" she whispered, grinning widely. I looked. The boys had discarded their digging and were now busily engaged doing something very complicated with a couple of pieces of string. We tactfully refrained from enquiring whether or not the shelter was ready for occupation.

Not long after the episode of the shelter, Sheila and I made a marvellous discovery. It all started when, playing near the stream, we spotted some fish swimming in the water. We ran to tell Aunty Doris but she said we "must be seeing things as there'd never been any fish in that pond". We persuaded her to 'come and see' and dragged her off to the edge of the stream where our 'fish' were still swimming away happily.

Aunty Doris peered into the depths. "Good gracious" she exclaimed "Well I never, they're not fish they're eels!" Sheila and I made a vain attempt to catch one. "Here, come out of it you two, you won't catch them like that, they're far too slippery. We'd better get some old cloths."

An hour or so later Aunty Doris had fished out a bowl full of squirming black eels. Sheila and I were delighted. We carried them carefully into the shed where Uncle Harry stored the potatoes, vegetables and spare mash along with all the garden tools and other miscellaneous impedimenta. Oh, the smell of that shed, it was glorious. The earthy smell of potatoes and old sacks mingled with the sweetness of the mash and the sharpness of apples all neatly wrapped and stored separately on trays in readiness for winter. From the beams hung strings of onions, bunches of mint, parsley and other useful herbs, adding their pungent odours to complete a perfect pot.-pourri of the countryside. Sheila and I thought it the perfect place in which to play 'fish shops'.

17

Our game went on for many days as we happily weighed and sold the 'fish' to each other. The eels must have been getting rather 'high' by now but we didn't notice, we were far too engrossed in our game. One morning, when we went into our 'shop', the eels had disappeared. "Gone back to the stream" said Aunty Doris when we enquired as to their whereabouts. Grown-ups can be very devious. Oh well, there were lots of other things to do.

Twice a week, Aunty Doris would sit at the table with me whilst I laboriously wrote a letter home. Mother kept these letters and, when she died a few years ago, I found one of them, a little yellow with age and frayed around the edges, but still legible.

In my letters I tried to recount as many of my activities as possible. The letter I found ended with me informing my parents that 'I would have to close now as it was time to put Peggy to bed'. Peggy, as my parents knew, was the goat kept tethered on the front lawn!

Every Wednesday morning the postman would arrive with an important delivery, just for me. We had a special arrangement, the postman and me. My parcel was never delivered in the conventional way through the letterbox. Instead, I would be woken by a gentle tapping on my bedroom window and then 'plop' the parcel would be dropped through the open window on to my bed. As soon as I had managed to rip off the outer covering, I would find "Tiny Tots" and "Chicks Own", my favourite comics, posted on to me by my parents. Later, when there was more time, Aunty Doris would read the stories to me and I would, once again, be enthralled by the adventures of the lovable characters I knew so well.

Once a week Aunty Doris made a trip into Chester to do her shopping. On the way we would stop at a little shop owned by a kindly lady called Mrs. Stubbs. Her shop was one of the old fashioned kind, packed with all sorts of goodies and delightful smells. There were large sacks of sugar from which she would weigh the required amount for each customer and then pack it into dark blue coned shaped bags. Big slabs of butter stood on the counter waiting to be cut and slapped into shape by the large wooden butter pats. Loose currants, sultanas and other dried fruit were also stored in big sacks and weighed out, individually, for each customer. Bacon was sliced on a large machine whilst you waited, each customer being asked "What number do you want it cut on?", the thickness of slice dependent upon the number you chose. Should cheese be on the shopping list then a small piece would be cut and offered so that you could taste it before buying. And always, either a free lollipop or a few sweets in a little twist of paper for me. I was entranced.

On then to Chester Market where the stalls were carefully laid out by the local market gardeners and traders. Crispy lettuce rubbed shoulders with fresh brown eggs, the bloom of that day's laying still on them. Slabs of home made butter and cheese piled high beside pink, juicy farm sausages. Jars of pickles and preserves flashed like jewels. Succulent oven-ready chickens sat alongside bowls of juicy red tomatoes. The freshly dug potatoes, with the rich dark Cheshire soil still clinging to them, lay alongside the carefully scrubbed carrots, turnips and swedes. On the other side of the hall the smell of freshly baked bread, cakes and biscuits suddenly made you realise how hungry you were. Chester market was crammed with good things to delight both the eye and the appetite. Home made sweets, herbal preparations, household goods, dress and curtain material, all were here for the asking.

Once our purchases were complete, we left the market and crossed over to a delightful little road that ran alongside the cathedral. The architecture here was like something straight out of Dickens. Pillars ran down the length of the pavement supporting the roofing that protected shoppers from the elements. All the shops had bow windows filled with all sorts of colourful and attractive goodies. I could visualise ladies in crinolines walking down the street, as I'm sure they must have done in the past, for Chester is one of our oldest Cities.

We stopped at a cake shop where we bought a large fruit cake and a box of fancy cakes and then, purchases complete, retraced our steps back towards the Town Hall and the big maroon and cream bus that would take us back to Blacon.

In all, I spent about three months at Blacon. Three months during which none of the horrific things we had anticipated happening in the Cities transpired. It was the 'phoney' war and, gradually, a feeling of hope that the bombing we had all feared would not now take place.

Parents began discussing the possibility of bringing their children home again and my parents, like many others, decided that I should return home.

One morning, a letter arrived from my parents and Aunty Doris told me that my father would come the following day and take me home with him. I greeted this news with some mixed feelings. Of course I wanted to go home and be with my parents again, but I knew I would miss so many things at Blacon. I wouldn't be able to play with Sheila and the other children. What about Peggy, the hens and Dorothy? Especially Dorothy; who would look after her? Aunty Doris reassured me that they would look after Dorothy and I could come over and see her whenever I wanted and, with that, I had to be content.

Once again my bags were packed and I was got ready, this time for my father's arrival. Oh what joy to see him coming up the path. I ran to meet him and he swept me up into his arms and hugged me. It was hard to believe that, only a few months ago, I had been so anxious to leave home and get away, now I was just as excited at the prospect of going home again with him. All my fears of war seemed to have magically evaporated.

After lots of goodbyes to Sheila and my friends, to Peggy and the hens, to Dorothy. Poor Dorothy, what was she going to do without me. I picked her up and hugged her with tears pricking the backs of my eyes whilst she, ungrateful creature, just squirmed and tried frantically to rid herself of my attentions.

Eventually it was time to leave. Father picked up my case as I gave Aunty Doris a special hug and then we were off, walking hand in hand down the path. Aunty Doris and Uncle Harry accompanied us to the gate and waved until we were out of sight.

I was on my way home to Liverpool.

Family group at "Rose Cottage"

20

CHAPTER 3

"Going Home"

3

It was December when I returned home to Liverpool and Christmas preparations were in full swing. The big stores were bright and colourful with paper decorations strung high above the heads of the eager, happy shoppers. Homes were gay with paper garlands, whilst imitation Christmas trees were brought out, dusted down and put into use, taking pride of place in the living rooms. In many ways, the war seemed a million miles away, or maybe the people subconsciously realised that this was the lull before the storm and determined to make the very best they could of this last Christmas before the privations began.

The ferry boat was crowded with people and I hung on to my father as it approached the Pier Head. After the usual bump as the fenders touched, there was a loud clatter as the gangplank was lowered and suddenly everyone was milling off the boat and on to the landing stage.

Although I had only been away three months, it was almost like coming back to a strange City. The doorways and windows of the Liver Buildings, the Cunard Building, the Town Hall and other major structures in the City were now safeguarded by piles of sandbags neatly stacked up against them.

I started to ply my father with the usual why's and what's and he, patient as always, tried to explain what the sandbags were, why the barrage balloons were flying above the Mersey, why the car headlights and bicycle lamps were fitted with black hoods and, at the same time, make it all sound quite matter of fact so I wouldn't be alarmed.

By now, of course, black-out restrictions were enforcable by law; street lighting was banned completely, traffic lights and vehicle indicators became tiny crosses of light, the rest of the bulb blotted out in black.

It was late in the afternoon and the sky was darkening rapidly as we neared home. Crossing roads had now become an extremely perilous operation for motorists found it difficult to see pedestrians in the black-out just as pedestrians found it difficult to see the approaching vehicles.

"Wait a minute now" my father warned as we waited to cross County Road. "Right, come on, all clear." We were across.

After the initial rapture of returning home, seeing my mother, being fussed over by our old faithful Fox Terrier, Billy, and re-discovering favourite toys and secret little hideaways, life quickly returned to normal and soon it was almost as though I'd never been away.

Most of the houses had, by now, taken on a new appearance for the windows had to be protected against the danger of flying glass and splinters due to bomb blast. Many women used a thick brown sticky tape.

"Can we have brown sticky paper on our windows" I asked my mother, much taken up by the artistic designs some women had evolved and secretly hoping to be allowed to do ours myself.

"No, we don't need that, I've got some of this net curtaining to glue on, it's safer" replied my ever practical mother. Disappointed, I had to forego all the plans for making weird and wonderful patterns that I had been so fondly harbouring.

My parents were now busily engaged filling the shop with Christmas stock. Mother dressed the window with brightly coloured crepe paper in green and red and a Christmas tree stood proudly in the centre. Around this was displayed all the toys that so many of the local children would be hoping to find in their stockings on Christmas morning. My father, meanwhile, strung brightly coloured calendars across the length and breadth of the shop and decorated the shelves to match the window.

Our 'Christmas Club' was in full swing and parcels and packages began to mount up in the shop overflowing into our living room as toys, books, annuals and chocolates were 'put away' in the Club. There was a wide selection to choose from, for a doll of good quality, sold at about 6/6d whilst dolls of all colours and sizes could be purchased from about 1/- to the most expensive at 5/-. A range of clockwork toys could be had from about 6d to 1/6d and a dozen Christmas Crackers sold for about 1/-. Whilst these prices might seem unbelievably cheap, it has to be remembered that wages were extremely low in those days. Excitement mounted as the big day grew nearer and nearer.

The local children, their noses pressed hard against the window, played their usual game outside the shop.

"I'm 'avin that"

"No you're not, I'm 'avin that"

"You're not, I said it first"

23

"Well I'm 'avin that then"

"I'm 'avin that as well".

It was the same every year. Whether or not they ever actually received their desires or, in fact, really wanted them in the first place did not matter. It was a good game, it was fun and that was all that really mattered.

By now my mother's thoughts, like most of the housewives, turned to food and the stocking up of the larder. There was, as yet, no shortage of food and the housewives made the most of it. Anything that didn't get eaten over Christmas could be put away, in case we went 'on the ration'. With Turkeys at 1/8d per lb, slab cake 1/-d, mince pies 1/-d a dozen and eggs 1d each, we were going to have a feast.

There were still a large number of children away from home and, although it was accepted that their hosts would share whatever they had with their small guests, the Lord Mayor of Liverpool made an appeal for £1,000 to augment the £2,000 voted by the Council to provide Christmas cheer for the school children away from home.

The Post Office was having its own problems and issued a 'Post Early for Christmas' plea. They were worried in case the black-out and call-up of men might interfere with their operations and everyone was asked to post early and in daylight hours, to ease their load.

Christmas Eve arrived at last and I spent most of my time happily engaged in wrapping my own presents to my mother and father and looking out parcels put away in the 'Club'. The shop was mad busy as parents, frantically trying to finish off the last of their Christmas shopping without the children observing what was being bought, called to collect their 'Clubs'.

Later, tucked up in bed and tingling with excitement, I tried desperately to catch sleep. Why, oh why is it so hard to go to sleep on Christmas Eve? I tossed and turned, worried in case HE came before I was asleep. It didn't bear thinking about. Happily HE never did.

Next morning, as soon as I awoke, I began poking around the bottom of the bed with a tentative foot. Suddenly it touched something heavy and lumpy. 'He's been, He's been'. Excitedly I began ripping the paper off the parcels. What a magical moment that is.

Later, presents opened and duly admired, we sat down to our Christmas dinner. Mother had bought a goose this year and in it came, golden brown and succulent. The juices ran down the crispy skin as she slid the knife in to carve the first slice. Roast potatoes, sprouts, sage and onion stuffing, apple sauce and rich brown gravy accompanied the slices of tender meat on our plates. We followed this with a rich Christmas Pudding and ended up replete and blown.

The festivities over, there were other joys to anticipate for the pantomime season was upon us. We had lots of pantomimes to choose from that year. The Empire was staging 'Robinson Crusoe' with Caryll & Mundy and Nita Croft, the Royal Court put on 'Goody Two Shoes' with Eddie Gray and Gwyneth Lascelles, whilst the Pavilion had those two great favourites, Arthur Lucan & Kitty McShane (better known to us as Old Mother Riley and Kitty) in 'The Old Woman Who Lived in a Shoe', and the Shakespeare starred another old favourite, Florrie Ford in 'Aladdin'.

My parents chose "The Old Woman Who Lived in a Shoe" and I happily joined in the singing, laughing, clapping and shouting with the rest of the children in the audience. For a few hours, we were transported to a different world, a world where there was no dark threat of war, no sandbags or stirrup pumps or any of the other impedimenta of war. However, when we finally left the theatre, the songs still ringing in our ears and stepped out into dark blacked-out streets, it was a salutory reminder that we were not living in normal times, no matter how much we might pretend, even for a few hours.

A steady trickle of children now began returning home and talk of re-opening the schools began. The Government took care to emphasise that this was not an invitation to parents to bring children back but, nevertheless, back they came. It seemed incredible that we had all worried so much about bomb attacks at the beginning of the war. Why, here we were four months later and nothing had happened. We were beginning to get a little more than complacent in our hope that it would carry on like this.

Education must have been a tremendous problem for the adults. We children would have been quite happy if the schools had remained closed as we were blissfully unaware of the effect this would have on our future lives. 40,000 children had been evacuated from Liverpool and there were still a large number at home. As more and more children returned, the authorities began preparations for a home teaching scheme in Bootle and a shift system in other schools. Eventually, the schools were gradually re-opened. But not yet. It was April before Arnot Street and Gwladys Street opened their doors and then only for the seniors.

One morning in January, I awoke to see soft white snowflakes falling steadily past the bedroom window.

"It's snowing, it's snowing" I shouted gleefully. It was bitterly cold, with a strong east wind blowing and already the snow was blowing into drifts of 3ft and 4ft.

"Can I go out?" I pleaded all morning. Eventually my mother relented and I dashed off to play in Ripon Street before she changed her mind.

We made a huge snowball by rolling it the length of the road until it was too big for us to move and there it stood in all its glory whilst we pelted each other with snowballs. Somebody's mother brought hot Oxo out to keep us warm, but we were so busy we didn't feel the cold. As we sipped our hot drinks, we heard that the adjoining Emery Street, had challenged us to a snowball fight. It was to be us against them and they'd be coming in about half an hour! No time to lose we began to build a big barricade across the centre of the road and stock up piles of snowballs in readiness. A look-out was posted to keep watch and, when the cry went up "They're coming!", we grabbed armfuls of snowballs and pelted each other happily.

Whilst we children were thoroughly enjoying ourselves, the adults were struggling to cope with the worst winter in Europe since 1860 and the worst winter in living memory in this country. On the night of 20th January, 1940, a temperature of 14.7 degrees fahrenheit was recorded in Liverpool, the lowest temperature for fifty years. Ice packs appeared in the River Dee, parts of the Mersey froze and rail and road services were completely dislocated. Tram tracks and points were packed with snow and ice and many services had to be discontinued. Standpipes were set up as 29,000 pipes burst and defects were caused to 220 mains. In Aigburth, two dozen people were forced to spend the night in five tramcars.

It was the same all over the country and the Army was called in to help clear railway lines between Manchester and Sheffield. Excavators were even brought in to try and clear some City streets and some trains were reported 'lost' in snowdrifts.

As the elements relented and conditions started to improve other problems were poised to take over.

Our parents were sombrely discussing the scuttling of the 'Graf Spey', the German pocket battleship in the harbour of Montevideo. Most of this went over our heads because we did not really understand what it was all about and were far more interested in our own pursuits. This momentous event was, however, pushed into the background when the survivors of the 'Altmark' returned. Once again, we didn't really realise what it was all about but, somehow or other, that they were heroes, we had no doubt.

Easter was approaching now and we looked forward to the advent of Spring. As at Christmas, most folk tried to make the most of the holiday and went off for day trips over the water to Thurstaston, New Brighton, Raby Mere and other local beauty spots.

Like most other children I had still not returned to school. Not that this worried me nearly as much as it worried my parents. Much to my disgust, however, Miss Sharpe, our Headmistress, decided to re-open the whole of our school after the Easter break.

Ah well, make the most of the holiday because very soon it would be 'back to school' for me.

The author with Terry.

The author with Billy.

CHAPTER 4

"Our School"

4

Spellow Lane School was a large three-storey house. The ground floor consisted of two large rooms divided by a wooden partition. The front room housed the seven to ten year olds, sub-divided into four classes, each working to a different syllabus. The back room housed the ten to fourteen year olds, sub-divided in a similar way.

From the front door a long hall ran alongside the two rooms leading into a smaller room which served as a Study for Miss Sharpe, our Headmistress. Off the Study was a kitchen where, in the winter months, our morning milk was heated. It also stored a large quantity of mugs for the use of the school at large, together with all the cleaning equipment.

Our milk was delivered in large containers rather than the small individual bottles supplied to the bigger schools and this was then poured into large jugs, one for each class.

The second floor consisted of a large double room in which Shorthand, Typing and Book-keeping was taught to any of the over-fourteens who wished to stay on and avail themselves of this 'Commercial Class' as we called it. Also on this floor was a bathroom — complete with bath, washbasin and lavatory this being the girl's toilet. The boys had to use an outside lavatory at the bottom of the back garden.

The top floor housed the babies classes. This, of course, presented a slight problem for it meant tiny legs having to climb several flights of stairs and being accompanied down whenever they had need to visit the lavatory. From the practical point of view of space, it made sense since the rooms were much smaller than the downstairs ones and there were not so many children in the babies classes as the senior ones. A strange offshoot from this arrangement was that we proudly claimed "I'm going down next term" when we reached seven years old, giving the impression to those 'not in the know' that we were being demoted rather than promoted.

Our school did not enjoy the luxury of electricity, so our lighting consisted of gas mantles, like many other houses at that time. These mantles were never very long lasting and when burnt out the complicated procedure of renewing them began. We would sit, arms folded, trying to look very responsible and trustworthy in eager anticipation of being chosen to help.

First, the teacher would fetch a small box, open it carefully and instruct the chosen child to remove the old mantle. This involved climbing up on top of the desk and carefully unhooking it. The new mantle would then be carefully handed up and great care had to be taken to ensure you did not touch the fragile white centre. After fitting, came the delicate process of lighting. The fitting resembled a pair of scales and was balanced with much the same delicate precision. A large bar stretched across the top and, on either side of this, a chain hung down with a ring attached to the bottom. The ring on one side had to be pulled down to bring forth the flow of gas and then a lighted taper applied. As soon as the flame met the flow of gas, it lit with a bang and then the two rings were adjusted to balance the flow. Once lit the new mantle had to 'settle in' and we suffered the indescribable smell that could last for anything up to half an hour.

We had no playground so, therefore, never had 'playtime'. Other compensations came our way, however, for when we arrived at school, we went straight into our classrooms. Unlike the larger schools, we never had to wait in the playground to assemble in lines and be marched in when the school bell rang. A definite advantage in inclement weather.

In order to make up for this lack of playtime, Miss Sharpe took the whole school to Swainsons every Friday afternoon. Swainsons was a large ballroom on the corner of Walton Lane and Cherry Lane and was used for adult dances. The highly sprung floor was polished and sprinkled with French chalk and we occupied ourselves sliding across the floor until brought to order by a loud blast on the whistle.

About 3.30 p.m. the mothers of the younger children would arrive to collect their offspring. We could see them watching us through the glass panes in the big double doors as they patiently waited outside. The older children were allowed an extra half-hour after the babies had gone home and then it was 'Take your partners for the last waltz' after which we would dive into the cloakroom to change our shoes, collect our coats and other belongings before setting off for home.

The equipment in our school would probably come somewhat as a surprise to many pupils today, for slates and slate pencils were still in use in the babies class. It was a big day indeed when you were promoted to pen and ink and we couldn't wait to pass this important piece of information on to our parents and show off in front of those still confined to using slates.

Our pens had wooden stems and loose nibs that fitted into a slot and had to be continually dipped into the inkpots that sat in small wells on our desks. The ink was of the powder variety which had to be reconstituted with water and the pots were refilled each day by the 'Ink Monitor', a much sought after job.

After such a long spell away from school it was surprising how quickly we fell back into the usual routine, only to be broken by air-raid practice and gas mask practice.

Gas mask practice took place in the class itself and was at the discretion of the teacher. Gas masks had to be carried wherever you went and we had little cardboard boxes in which to keep them. Attached to the box was a large string so that they could be slung over the shoulder like a shoulder bag.

Air-raid practice was a different matter altogether. These took place regularly and we would never be warned in advance but rather be brought up sharply in the middle of a lesson by the loud ringing of the school handbell.

Although these were difficult times for both teachers and pupils, discipline was never allowed to slip. A cane always hung on the wall of Miss Sharpe's Study, a salutory reminder to any would-be young sinner. This was put into use on several occasions, the malefactor always being sent to the Headmistress.

Discipline was very strong in those days and teachers were treated with much respect. The thought of having to be sent to the Headmistress for a scolding, let alone a caning, was often more than enough to deter any young offender. Miss Sharpe was a stern and imposing figure.

Forms of punishment were metered out according to the deed. When one hears some of the language used by youngsters today it seems difficult to believe that, at that time, swearing was one of the unpardonable sins. Miss Sharpe would not countenance it under any circumstances. On one occasion when a youngster was overheard committing this dreadful deed, the news swept through the school.

"Jimmy Mason swored"

"He didn't"

"He did, honest, Miss Johnson heard him"

"What did he say?"

"Don't know"

This last with great disappointment, for we were all agog to know just what the dreadful word was.

We were aware of the punishment for this particular 'crime' and we waited, arms folded and silent as the preparations began. First, the big wooden partitions between the two lower rooms were opened out. We were then told to squeeze up and make room for the other classes that were to join us. This was something to be witnessed by the school at large. Silently they filed in and took their places. A table was brought in from the kitchen and on this was placed a bowl of water, a bar of carbolic soap and a towel. Preparations completed, the door opened and Miss Sharpe solemnly entered escorting the small sinner to the table.

We sat and watched as he was instructed to wash his mouth out with carbolic soap. Then, his ordeal over, Miss Sharpe led him out and a burst of nervous chatter exploded throughout the room.

"Silence" thundered one of the teachers "Back to your classrooms." We fell silent immediately and obeyed.

We did not have school dinners at that time. Most of the children went home for dinner, whilst those who lived too far away brought sandwiches which they ate at their desks, hot drinks being provided from the kitchen. If anyone wanted to run off excess energy during the lunch hour, which consisted of two hours, they had to make do with either the front or back garden.

A two-hour dinner break may seem rather long but I always found it passed quite quickly, too quickly in fact. Once a month I would arrive home to find several commercial travellers in our shop. Strictly against all the courtesy rules of the road, these four actually arranged to meet. The purpose of this meeting extraordinaire was purely to discuss the merits of their particular football teams and, as soon as they had all assembled, our next door neighbour, Mrs. Close, would come and join the group. It was an uproarious time with much good natured bantering until, having settled the probable league positions to their satisfaction, they would disperse, arranging to meet the same time, same place, next month.

Once school was over for the day, I would be allowed to play out for a few hours in Ripon Street. There were quite a few children, both boys and girls living in Ripon Street and we girls tended to play together and leave the boys to their more boisterous games. Occasionally, however, we would join forces to play 'Relievo'. For this, one child would be chosen as 'it' by means of a very serious ceremony of 'counting out'. Standing in a circle, holding clenched fists in front of us, one child would go round chanting 'one potato, two potato, three potato, four, five potato, six potato, seven potato more' touching a fist at each count. The one whose fist was touched on the final count of 'more' was out and then the counting would begin again until, finally, only one child was left to be 'it'.

After the counting-out process was complete we would scatter leaving 'it' to count to ten and then, with a shout of 'coming, ready or not', 'it' would try to catch as many of us as possible. Once caught you had to stand still with your arms outstretched. If another managed to run up and touch you, without getting caught, you were 'relieved' and could run off again. 'It' not only had to catch everyone but guard the ones already caught in case they got 'relieved' and the whole lot could be running free again. We played this endlessly and never tired of it.

A lot of our games were dependent upon the seasons. Top and Whip was favoured in the Spring, skipping in the Summer — when we would beg lengths of clothes line from our mothers and, stretching them across the width of the street, take turns at turning the rope whilst others skipped to the rhymes we chanted. One of our favourites was:-

I am a Girl Guide dressed in blue,
These are the actions I must do,
Salute to the King, bow to the Queen,
Stand at attention, stand at ease.

We suited our actions to the words whilst skipping and, finally, had to end up legs astride the rope 'at ease'. There were many more rhymes such as this and we skipped for hours on end happily wearing out our shoe leather.

We played 'ollies' in the road, rolling the tiny glass marbles along trying to hit someone elses. If successful, you were then allowed to take their 'olly' and add it to your own collection. These small 'ollies' were highly prized, some more than others, dependent upon the patterns and colours of the markings inside them.

The paving stones would be marked out in big squares numbered one to ten in order to play hopscotch. It was essential to choose the right place for this game otherwise you were in danger of incurring the wrath of an indignant housewife for chalking on her nice clean pavement. So houseproud were some of the women that they even scrubbed the paving stones outside their houses as well as the front door steps.

When it rained, this would put a stop to our games but not to our playing together. Huddled up in somebody's 'lobby' we would sit making clothes for our dolls. We fashioned these out of all sorts of scraps of materials and, although some of the little girls were very adept with needle and thread, sadly I was not one of them.

"Are you coming to Band of Hope tonight?" Doreen, one of my friends, asked.

"What's Band of Hope?" I asked.

"It's the gear, they have a Magic Lantern Show" came the reply.

I was none too sure about this, it was something new to me, but nevertheless I ran off home to seek permission.

After asking me who I was proposing to go with, where it was to be held, what time it finished and all the other questions parents are wont to ask, I was granted permission. Five o'clock that evening saw me happily tripping off to 'Band of Hope' with all the others.

As we walked down Goodison Road towards the little Mission Hall we could see lots of other children converging on the building. We lined up outside, paid our pennies to the lady at the door and went into a large room with wooden benches running the width. We found a bench and sat down excitedly. A large man stood at the front and began to talk about missionary work in Africa and other far away countries and then went on to extol the evils of drinking alcohol. After this we stood and sang a hymn accompanied by the lady on the piano and then, suddenly, the room was plunged into darkness. The Magic Lantern Show was to begin.

None of the pictures moved and each had to be changed by means of taking a large square plate out of the back of the projector and sliding another into its place. It was very much like an antiquated version of the present day slide projector. Occasionally the man made a mistake and the picture would appear upside down, this would be greeted with much giggling and chattering and, whilst he corrected his error, the lady would shout at us to be quiet. Band of Hope did not last very long and we were soon leaving the Hall and making our way home.

"Did you enjoy it?" mother asked when I arrived home.

"I'd rather go to the pictures" I replied.

My mother laughed "You've been spoilt" she said.

CHAPTER 5

"Spies, Rations and Careless Talk"

5

After one of the worst winters in living memory, signs of Spring arrived at last. The trees in the park were full of fat, sticky buds waiting to burst into leaf, whilst clumps of daffodils stood waving their heads in the fresh breeze that blew down from the Mersey. We looked forward to the long light summer nights ahead, little knowing what they would bring.

There were other changes, apart from those provided by nature. The winds of war were blowing hard across Europe and the authorities were only too well aware that, as each day passed, the giant Nazi war machine was creeping nearer and nearer to our shores. Defence arrangements were going ahead swiftly and the parks and roads began to bloom with more than daffodils.

On our first visit to Walton Hall Park that Spring, we saw that an Ack-Ack gun had been installed in the big field with a large barrage balloon flying above it. On our way to the park I saw large concrete pyramid shapes and rolls of barbed wire stored at the side of road junctions. When I asked my parents what these were I was told they were to block the movement of enemy troops should there be an invasion. Concrete pill boxes with tiny round apertures only big enough for a gun nozzle to poke through stood ready to be manned in an emergency. Our defences were being prepared and obviously my parents saw no reason to hide this fact from me. Strangely enough we children accepted it as though it was a normal occurrence. Without realising the fact, we had gradually been conditioned to accepting that we were at war and it was now almost a normal part of our childhood.

Earlier in the week, my father had had occasion to visit one of the warehouses in town and had taken me with him. Our our way home we walked to the Pier Head to catch a No. 21 tram. Looking out over the river, we could see barrage balloons flying high over the ships at anchor in the Mersey.

"Can we go down on the Landing Stage, you can see them better down there?" I asked.

We walked down and stood by the railings. Just then a man sidled up to my father.

"Are there any men in them?" he asked.

"No, they're filled with gas" my father replied, and went on to explain their purpose to the stranger. I felt safe and secure as I held his hand. My father knew all the answers I thought.

Instead of going for the 'messages' on a Saturday morning, I now went for the 'rations'. Food rationing had begun in January, 1940, and my parents had buff coloured ration books, whilst mine was blue. The under fives and expectant mothers were given green books that allowed them extra supplies of high protein foods and an allowance of orange juice and vitamins.

Shopping was fairly easy for there was no real choice. Each family registered with one shop and it was merely a question of handing over the ration books and receiving your allocation. Most of the time these consisted of; two ounces of butter, four of margarine and two of lard for each person. In addition you got; two ounces of cheese, four of bacon, two ounces of tea and twelve ounces of sugar. Canned goods were on a points system and this, at least, left a certain amount of choice to the consumer.

When it came to getting the meat ration, mother preferred to shop herself for, with a ration of 1/10d per person per week, it was essential to choose wisely in order to make the most of the meagre amount allowed. Poultry and fish were 'off the ration', as were sausages and offal, but these were in very short supply and any shop fortunate enough to have such commodities on sale soon discovered a large number of housewives waiting in an orderly fashion outside. The British habit of queueing had begun.

Petrol rationing had been in existence since October, 1939, but this did not bother many families as few had cars in those days. Those that were fortunate enough to own a vehicle got sufficient petrol to cover 200 miles per month by car, whilst businessmen got a supplementary allowance which varied according to the size of engine; 4 gallons for an Austin 7, 10 gallons for a Rolls Royce. There were no brand names of petrol only 'pool'. In July 1940, the manufacture of new cars was stopped and in 1942 allowances for private motoring stopped altogether. Motorists drained their sumps and kept the car raised on wood blocks for the duration. Some did experiment with gas bags on the roof and very strange sights these proved to be. They were neither efficient nor popular and were soon discarded.

One of the highlights of April was the Grand National run at Aintree Racecourse. Probably because it was a local event as well as a national institution it was always a major topic of conversation. Most families had a modest bet and 'sweeps' were organised to add to the excitement. Even the children were included and, once the list of runners was published in the paper, we would pick our horse by means of closing our eyes and sticking a pin in the list.

This year there was doubt as to whether or not the race would, in fact, be run. In September, 1939, the racecourse had been taken over by the authorities but, Mrs. Mirabel Topham, the owner, had fought bitterly to rid herself of her unwanted guests and had finally won. She was not so successful in later attempts for, after the fall of France, the racecourse was finally taken over to billet troops. As this was to be the last race for the 'duration' nearly everyone placed a bet. As usual, most people were disappointed and only the lucky ones, who backed a horse by the name of 'Bogskar', rejoiced as it romped home past the winning post.

By now the full force of the propaganda campaign was in operation. We children realised, as much as the adults, that no help must be given, however unwillingly, to the enemy.

"Careless talk costs lives" the placards on the hoardings screamed down to us. "Be like Dad, keep Mum" — I long puzzled over the meaning of that one.

With all the rumours regarding the sighting of parachutists landing in various places in all sorts of guises, we children soon evolved a new game — searching for spies. We had great fun pretending someone was a spy and trying to keep them under close surveillance until, bored by their lack of suspicious activity, we moved on to seek out another innocent victim to follow.

There was, as yet, little disruption to our normal lives for we were still able to play out, we were back at school and were, to a great extent, oblivious of the tremendous happenings in Europe. These things were left to the grown-ups to worry about, we were too busy with our latest craze, making pom-poms.

Our milk was delivered to the dairy in large churns which stood on the floor by the counter. The milk was ladled out into the glass bottles or large white jugs brought by the customer. Fortunately my mother favoured the milk bottles and I was able to collect the cardboard tops from them. Once the small round centre was removed, wool was carefully threaded around two tops placed together and after they had been covered with several rows of wool, the outer edge was cut with a pair of scissors and a piece of wool carefully threaded round the centre and drawn up tight. The result was a brightly coloured pom-pom.

I looked forward eagerly to my comics each week. By now, I had progressed from 'Chicks Own' and 'Tiny Tots' to 'Radio Fun' and

'Film Fun'. The characters in our comics had undergone changes so that they now reflected the time in which we were living. Stories of 'spies' abounded and the Germans were depicted as being rather foolish figures who were continually being thwarted by all our favourite characters.

We, of course, were completely unaware that this was quite a clever psychological move on the part of the creators of these stories who hoped that, by making the Germans figures of fun, they would remove a good deal of the dread and fear from our minds. It worked better than they could possibly have hoped for we lapped it up. We had no great fear of the Germans and often discussed what we would do if they ever did invade.

"I'd hit him over the head with a shovel" vowed one brave lad.

"I'd get my mother's brush and shove him away" said another.

"Well, I'd kick him and stamp on his foot" decided a girl.

"I'd get the poker".

This might sound foolish now, but we'd seen all our favourite characters in our comics dealing with the Germans in this way and our ideas were not original but merely copies of what we had read. What a marvellous job they did in allaying our fears and making us feel brave and able to cope.

Our parents reading matter told a completely different story however, for they were reading, with heavy hearts, the accounts of the battle waging for Norway and Denmark and how the British were busy laying mines in the sea around their coasts. The cartoons did try to portray a lighter side by showing Hitler about to take a bath and suddenly finding a mine in it — the caption reading *"There's no telling where the British navy will lay them next."*

We were kept busy at school collecting waste paper and pounced eagerly on every bit we could find, storing it up in large bags. Liverpool Corporation Health Committee decided to award £5 as a prize to the school collecting the most waste comprising paper, bones, old clothes and other salvage material.

Scrap was being collected avidly now and one of the greatest needs was for metal. I had a much beloved blue tricycle which I used to ride up and down the back yard. However, when a large van appeared in City Road collecting old pans, kettles, buckets and anything that might be of use, my tricycle had to go.

"Don't you fret love, this'll make a fine mast for a battleship" the man confidently assured me as he carried it away.

Park railings disappeared and the small railings around the houses, all to the same cause — the 'War Effort'.

"Will Daddy have to go in the army?" I asked my mother one morning as we set the table for breakfast.

"No, I don't think so, he's too old" Mother replied.

This was something that had been worrying me now for some time as most of my friend's fathers had been 'called up' and were now in either the Army, Navy or Air Force. The age for call-up had been extended to cover all men between the ages of 19 and 36 but, as my father was over the age limit and had fought in the first World War, it was unlikely that he would be called. Nevertheless, he and the other older men 'did their bit' by taking on work that the younger men had had to leave. My father returned to his job in the printing trade later that year.

The families of the men who were away, waited eagerly for letters bringing them news. All letters to and from the armed forces were now opened by the 'Official Censor', read carefully and any information that might be of use to the enemy 'blue-pencilled' out to make it completely illegible. They were then carefully re-sealed, stamped with the Censor's seal and sent on their way.

Much fun was made of this censorship by Jack Warner in a programme called 'Garrison Theatre'. Part of his act was to read out a letter from his imaginary brother 'Syd' who was supposedly away in the forces. It was full of 'blue-pencil' crossings out and he made it sound hilariously funny. Having no television in those days, the radio and the pictures were our major sources of entertainment.

The Germans were busy with their propaganda machine as well. A British man living in Germany was recruited to broadcast to this country telling us, in menacing nasal upperclass tones, such as he thought we had a right to hear. Usually these were details of bombing raids over this country. He was quickly dubbed 'Lord Haw-Haw' and, although at first, some people began to wonder if there was any truth in his statements he lost all credibility when he announced that 'Heavy bombing had taken place, displaying the target accuracy of the Luftwaffe, when hundreds of bombs had been dropped at random' . He became a figure of fun and we children mimicked him by holding our noses with finger and thumb and reciting "Jairmany calling, Jairmany calling" his own call sign, whilst giggling and laughing at each other. 'Lord Haw-Haw' or, to give him his correct name, William Joyce, was brought for trial as a traitor and hanged at the Tower of London when the war in Europe was over.

"As if we haven't got enough to put up with" moaned one disgruntled old man to my mother, who was busy serving him with an ounce of thick twist. "3d on an ounce of tobacco, it's disgusting. A man's entitled to a decent smoke."

"Never mind your old tobacco, what about this Purchase Tax they're introducing" rejoined a spirited woman standing next to him. "That's going to affect everything we buy".

I decided to go out and play and leave them to their discussions on the latest Budget. The fact that there was to be a new tax and that Income Tax was to be increased from 7/-d in the £ to 7/6d, a penny a pint was to be put on beer, 1/9d on a bottle of whisky and increases on postage, postal orders and telephone calls were to be made didn't interest me in the slightest.

My main interest, at the moment, like most of the youngsters in the area, was the fact that reinforced concrete street shelters were being erected. Workmen had arrived in all the side streets off City Road. Those who were lucky enough to have wide entries at the back like Luxmore Road, Keith Avenue and Cowley Road, had their shelters built in the entries. We thought they would be perfect for playing in but our hopes were soon dashed when this idea was firmly squashed by our elders.

The reason the government had speeded up their plans to build street shelters was the news that Holland and Belgium had been attacked. It was only after Winston Churchill took over as Prime Minister on 10th May, 1940, and the schools were opened on a Saturday morning to facilitate a new evacuation of children, should the need arise, that I began to suspect the war was not going well for us.

I had no wish to be evacuated again and began to get more than a little concerned as to whether or not I would have to go away. It was somewhat strange that, when the war started, I had been so eager to get away and now, amidst all the preparations for an invasion of this country and the real danger of bomb attacks, my fears had gone and all I wanted to do was stay at home with my parents. Both assured me that I was not going away and many parents made the same decision. Apparently they had been told they could register their children to be removed from high priority areas in the event of heavy air attacks: 1,000 parents registered their children; 80,000 did not and Liverpool was considered a high priority area.

Looking back now, as an adult with all the facts to hand, it is not difficult to see why there was such concern. The British

Expeditionary Force was stranded on the beaches at Dunkirk but no-one, at that time, knew of the massive armada that was to go out and bring them home. That was information that would most certainly have been of use to the enemy and it was carefully and successfully shrouded in secrecy until June 4th, when news started coming through that over 1,000 small ships had brought more than 335,000 British and French troops safely back to our shores.

In addition to this, on 10th June, Italy decided to join in the War and become an ally of Hitler. This news caused great consternation for the thousands of Italians living in this country as they waited to see what the Home Office would say about their position. Rumours abounded saying that certain families were Italians when they were, in fact, naturalised British subjects, many of whom had already registered for military service under the National Service Armed Forces Act of 1939 and were waiting to be called up. So rife were these rumours that many of these unfortunate families had to resort to putting notices in the local paper to this effect, whilst threatening to institute legal proceedings against anyone stating otherwise. Some had their windows broken as bricks were thrown by irate and irresponsible members of the public wishing to vent their anger on 'unwanted aliens'.

On 17th June, 1940, France stopped fighting. Britain and the Empire stood alone against the mighty force of Hitler. We determined we would not be beaten, we would fight to the last. The Battle of Britain had begun.

PHOTOGRAPHIC SECTION ONE

"Today's Walton"

Walton Lane.

"The Lodge", Walton Lane.

46

Walton Hall Park.

Emery Street.

Spellow Lane.

Ripon Street.

Cowley Road.

Frodsham Street.

49

Goodison Road.

The Mission Hall, Goodison Road.

Keith Avenue.

Dyson Street.

Stopgate Lane.

City Road, looking up from St. Luke's Church.

The 'Brew', City Road.

City Road, looking down from the 'Brew'.

St. Luke's Church, City Road.

Luxmore Road.

CHAPTER 6

"Under the Stairs"

6

The fall of France meant invasion was now imminent. Only the few miles of the English Channel now separated us from the full force of Hitler's army. Look-outs scanned the length of the Channel for the first signs of a sea attack whilst, throughout the rest of the country, the sky was watched for parachutes. Church bells were silenced and, from now on, would only ring to signal invasion.

The government issued official advice to the public on what to do if the Invasion came. All vehicles were to be immediately immobilised so that the enemy could not use them for transport. Bicycle chains were to be removed and all tyres let down for the same reason. Strangers, asking for directions, were to be given no information. Road blocks would be established and the pill-boxes armed and manned. Civilians would be requested to stay off the streets and ignore all rumours.

There was no mass evacuation at this time as there had been last September. Most of the children had returned and both they and their parents were content for them to stay. A plan was drawn up to send British children abroad to Canada, South Africa, Australia and New Zealand, whilst America was seeking a way of modifying their immigration laws in order to admit a hundred thousand British children.

The newspapers, of course, were full of advice to their readers and very soon we all became quite knowledgeable about the different types of aeroplanes used by both the British and the Germans.

"Here, that's my Spitfire, give it me back"

"You haven't got the wings on right"

"Yes he has, here let's see it fly again"

The boys had a new game and fashioned their planes out of paper and cardboard from the information they got in comics and newspapers. As far as we girls were concerned it was just boy's stuff and we were content to leave them to it and concentrate on our own more peaceful activities.

Khaki, Air Force Blue and Navy uniforms were by now becoming a familiar sight on our streets as more and more men were recruited into the Forces. Sadly, after Dunkirk, a new uniform came to be seen, the Royal Blue of the wounded.

It was difficult to ignore the young men in blue struggling along the street on crutches or swathed in bandages. Everyone wanted to help but most were sensible enough to know that it was practical help that was needed not just kind words.

Much to our delight, our Headmistress decided to organise a concert to entertain the wounded in hospital. The idea was to try it out in Walton Hospital and, if successful, take it round to wherever the wounded were.

We began practising with great enthusiasm. Each class was given a simple song and dance routine to learn, some were parodies set to well known tunes. My favourite was the one set to the tune of 'Rule Brittania'. I cannot remember all the words now, but the last line "Eggs, are never, never, never quite new laid" was quite unforgettable.

The big partitions between the two downstairs rooms were folded back and we all assembled there once a week. Soon the room was resounding with the sound of feet pounding out the Sailor's hornpipe whilst, what in today's terminology might be called a backing group, squeaked away on tin whistles hopelessly losing the race to keep up with the piano accompaniment.

Some of the acts were extremely good and there was quite a lot of genuine talent amongst the children. Others were not so good whilst a few, myself included, were quite unable to carry a tune at all.

Sadly the concert never came to fruition as the authorities considered we were too young to enter the hospitals.

Whilst we were busy with our concert, our parents were anxiously watching the situation in Europe. The wireless became all-important.

Our wireless was run on electricity but many still used 'accumulators' and these had to be 'charged' every so often. There was a shop in City Road solely for this purpose and a good business they did. The old 'accumulators' would be taken in and exchanged for a fully 'charged' one and then the old one would be 're-charged' in readiness for the next customer. It was a continuous circle as there was always someone, sixpence in hand, waiting for another as their old ones 'ran out'.

Weather wise it seemed we were going to have a lovely summer, for the days began to get hot and hazy. The sky was a clear blue with puffy cottonwool clouds floating overhead. During half-term, I went into town with mother on one of her visits to the warehouse.

We walked down Ripon Street and Arnot Street and caught a 21 tram which would take us along Scotland Road and eventually into Whitechapel. As the tram progressed its shaky way through Everton and into Scotland Road, I played my usual game — counting the 'Mary Ellens'.

'Mary Ellens' were ladies who all dressed alike in long black skirts with white aprons tied across the front and a huge black shawl wrapped around their shoulders. On their feet they wore black boots or shoes. Their hair was dressed in a large bun to help balance the bundles of washing, or baskets, they carried on their heads.

Often, I would count up to seventy or eighty in the short while it took to travel along Scotland Road. On the way home, I counted the number of pubs, usually one to each street corner.

When we arrived in Whitechapel, we would head straight for Conlons the newspaper warehouse. Downstairs all the business in connection with newspapers and magazines was conducted. Long trestle like tables were set up in rows the length of the room and on these were set all the magazines and newspapers. The heavy smell of newsprint and paper pervaded the whole building and the large amount of paper seemed to muffle all sounds. Soon we were climbing the stairs to the Stationery Department. I found this fascinating for it sold everything from paper clips to reading books. If ever I needed a new exercise book for school, this was the place to find it. Always when getting a new book I would promise myself that this one was going to be kept especially neat and tidy. My good resolution usually lasted about a quarter of the way through and then gradually faded away until, on reaching the last page, I would once again vow that the next one would be different.

After we left the warehouse, I was often able to persuade my mother to accompany me to "The Wizard's Den" in Moorfields. It was a magical shop, full of jokes, masks and tricks. The window was jam-packed with a selection of all these goods and it was difficult to find a space to look in for almost everyone wanted to gaze in the window. Bowler hatted businessmen rubbed shoulders with small scruffy urchins, the attraction of the "Wizard's Den" was universal.

We had yet to experience 'air-raids' as such, but the possibility was growing day by day. My father went down into the cellar below the shop and cleared under the stairs in readiness. Mother took some chairs down and tried to squeeze them in for there was little enough room under the stairs but it was supposed to be the safest part of the house to shelter during a raid. We had done all we could.

Arrangements were in hand for us to have a proper reinforced concrete and brick shelter built in the main part of the cellar, but we had to wait our turn for the builders were working overtime to try and keep up with the demand.

On 25th June, 1940, we heard, with dread in our hearts, the intermittant wailing of the siren, loud and clear across the city.

"Down under the stairs" ordered my father and we ran down and huddled there together.

It was dusty and the walls were flaking. The old whitewash brushed off onto our clothes as we scrambled in.

"Never mind that" said my father as I tried to brush it off my sleeve "just squeeze in".

We sat waiting, but thankfully nothing happened. It was thought that enemy planes had been sighted approaching Liverpool, but they had either turned away or our own fighter planes had managed to chase them off.

It was difficult to get news of what was happening in other parts of the country for the obvious reasons of security. Later, however, we heard that about a hundred planes had attacked the East coast in raids and, for the first time, Nazi bombers had been shot down over British soil. The front line was to be no distant battlefield. It was here on our own shores. All England and its citizens were in the first line of defence now.

Two days later the sirens went again and we huddled back under the stairs. This time, two incendiary bombs fell on the City. It looked as though it was going to be a 'flaming' June in more ways than the weather. Again, on the 28th they came, and six bombs were dropped. We waited anxiously over the next few days but, thankfully, it seemed they were not coming again. Little did we know what really was in store for us.

Hitler was now boasting that he would be in London by 15th August, we determined he would not. Everyone joined in the war effort wholeheartedly. The jobs vacated by the men who had been conscripted into the Forces began to be taken over by the women and older men. Women and girls were going into the armed forces the same as the men, but those with very young children were exempt. The older women went into the factories to make munitions, manned the tramcars and undertook whatever jobs they could. My father arranged to go back to his old job in the printing industry whilst my mother took over the running of the shop.

"I wonder what your Dad would say if I got a pair of those?"

Mother and I were out shopping in County Road and we had stopped to look in Hughes's window. They had a big display of ladies slacks in the window — 'Warm and comfortable and easy wear for the shelter' the advertisement said. "Come on, I think I'll get a pair" my mother decided.

Women who had never worn trousers before were now buying slacks as fashions began to change. People dressed for practical purposes now rather than sartorial elegance. Headscarves became popular and were worn in a variety of ways, especially by those women who worked on munitions, for they kept their hair neat and tidy and well away from the machinery.

Mother was pleased with her slacks and very practical they were too.

"Good idea" my father approved "You want to get her a pair as well"

I was over the moon when I heard him say this.

"Can I, can I mummy, can I have a pair like yours?"

"They don't make them in your size" she protested.

"It wouldn't take you long to make a pair for her, would it?" my father said, knowing only too well my mother's expertise at dressmaking.

"No, I suppose not. We'll have to see" mother replied.

I got my slacks.

The face of the City was changing yet again, for now we were being asked to 'Dig for Victory'. In other words, make as much use of whatever land you had for growing food. It wasn't much use asking us to 'Dig for Victory', we only had a back yard. The Ministry of Agriculture got power to use private parks, race courses and golf courses for the cultivation of food, if necessary. Football grounds were excluded and were to be kept for 'keep fit' purposes should it be necessary to cancel competitive football until after the war was over.

July came and on the 2nd, the sirens sounded again. This time we heard the enemy planes overhead, the guns fired but thankfully no bombs were dropped. After this there was a brief respite until the 15th, when again we had to scuttle for shelter. Once again the guns fired but no bombs were dropped. There were four more raids on Liverpool during July but all were of a minor nature and we entered August well aware of our air-raid drill.

"Here, go and put this up on the wall somewhere, there's a good girl" Mrs. Close said, as she passed a piece of paper over the counter to me.

I must have looked a bit unsure.

"It's alright, it's only the fire-watching rota for your Dad" she said by way of explanation.

Ah, now I knew what she was talking about.

Firewatching rotas were drawn up for each street and each Works. The neighbours got together and decided which nights they would be on duty and for how many hours and then a written sheet was drawn up and given to each person. Ours was pinned up on the back of the door into the shop so we would always know who was on duty and where.

During the first part of August, the siren sounded eight times as we thankfully took refuge under the stairs. Soon the workmen arrived to build our shelter. It was erected in the centre of the cellar itself, right under the shop floor. There were two exits; one that also served as an entrance and a special steel door at the far end that was opened by means of turning the wheel to remove the metal casing. This latter would bring us out under the iron grid in the street and, hopefully, if the house was destroyed, enable us to be rescued.

The shelter complete, my parents decided to bring my big double bed down in the hope that I might be able to sleep through some of the raids. I, like thousands of other children, was now sleeping in my parents room, on a camp bed at the side of theirs.

Our shelter was completed just in time, for on 20th August, one hundred incendiaries rained down on Liverpool in the worst raid on the City so far. Even worse was to come, for on the night of the 28th and 29th, we had the longest raid of the war so far. It lasted several hours and hundreds of incendiaries were dropped over the City. The whole sky was illuminated so brightly that it seemed to attract wave after wave of bombers like moths round a candle.

My parents were much concerned that I should not be afraid and, whenever we had to go into the shelter, we played games. Lexicon became a favourite for it was easy to play and consisted of making up words. Each card was printed with a letter of the alphabet and you could either make up your own word or add to the ones already down. My father began to put down words that were obviously incorrectly spelt in order to make me laugh. KOF would appear to my howl of protest that you didn't spell 'cough' like that and then I would see my father winking at my mother. Mother joined in this charade and put her own ill-spelt words down whilst my father would protest and say "Hey, hey, we'll have none of that there here, thank you very much" and make her retrieve them. This ploy worked to some extent but when the guns roared from the nearby parks and the scream of bombs and explosions became too loud I would ask anxiously,

"Are they overhead?"

"No, no, they're miles away yet" was the reply I always got.

I think we all knew the truth, for the sound of the German planes was unmistakable. They sounded very different from 'ours'. The steady whirring burr of British planes meant security, whilst the intermittent throbbing of German planes meant they were very near and danger was imminent.

One night, during a fairly heavy raid, we were sitting playing cards when, suddenly, mother jumped up and disappeared upstairs. We waited, wondering where she had gone.

"What on earth's your mother doing?" my father mused. I wondered the same thing.

The guns were firing away outside and we began to get anxious.

"I don't know, stay there and I'll go and see what she's up to" my father said.

I strained my ears to see if I could hear what was happening upstairs.

"You can't stay up here in the middle of all this. Now come and get back in the shelter" I heard my father saying.

No-one came.

I listened harder and heard my parents raised voices as father tried to persuade mother to come back, I couldn't make out what was going on.

Finally I heard my father say "For goodness sake, it's not going to harm you, get back down".

Footsteps on the stairs and both my parents returned.

Father sat down with a look of sheer exasperation, whilst mother looked very apprehensive and none too happy.

What on earth was the matter I wondered.

"Mummy, where've you been?" I asked, unable to contain my curiosity any longer.

Mother did not answer, but kept looking around her.

Father answered for her — "You're mother thought she saw a mouse"

CHAPTER 7

"It's Raining Shrapnel and Bombs"

7

Autumn crept upon us surreptitiously. The summer was almost over and we began to take for granted all the enormous change it had brought. We were now geared up to war and all its dreadful realities. There had been no August/Bank Holiday as such, time could not be spent on such frivolities, the loss of production in the factories would have been too great and we accepted this without question. The 'phoney war' was over and we were now plunged into the heart of the conflict with the air attacks on our City.

Our shelter was strong and well built, and gave me a feeling of security and safety. As soon as the siren sounded and we were within the confines of the solid brick walls, I knew we would be safe. No matter the intermittent droning of enemy planes getting nearer and nearer, the crack of the guns and the tremendous, terrifying explosions as the bombs fell, we were safely cocooned in our own little nest.

The sirens began their wailing early in the evening, often before the workers had returned home. My mother would watch anxiously for my father, worried in case he got 'caught' in a raid on the way home, for he now worked in the City centre.

We kept a primus stove in the shelter and mother would prepare the evening meal, set it to cook and then, when the sirens started, we would dash to the shelter and finish the cooking on the Primus stove. When the all-clear finally sounded, we would carry everything back upstairs, wash up and set a tray in readiness for the next onslaught.

Mother would put me to bed and a few hours later, I would feel my father gently shaking me and whispering "Come on love, wake up, the siren's gone". Sleepily, I would try and rouse myself as he picked me up in his arms and carried me down to the shelter where we would spend the next few hours playing Lexicon and listening to the dreadful holocaust outside.

On 4th September, we sat in the shelter as wave after wave of heavy droning bombers attacked Liverpool. The first wave dropped flares which lit up the whole area like Blackpool Illuminations. The succeeding wave of bombers, following in their wake, showered hundreds of incendiary bombs down on us. The whistle of bombs made us stop what we were doing and wait, almost too scared to breathe, to see how near they would fall. From the shelter we could hear the sound of shouting in the street and the heavy tread of men running to and fro as they called to each other giving instructions. There was no need to ask "Are they overhead?" for the heavy brr-brr the engines told us that all too clearly.

We tried to carry on playing our game, but the cards scattered on the floor as the high explosives thundered down causing the whole house to shudder and shake after each terrifying explosion.

After many long hours, the 'all clear' finally sounded and we thankfully returned upstairs, me to bed, my parents and the other adults to inspect the damage and make safe whatever they could.

The next night we were back in the shelter shortly after dark as waves of enemy planes swept overhead. The night raiders stayed over Liverpool until nearly dawn and, when they finally departed, they left in their wake the largest number of casualties yet. All the damage was to civilian property, no military objectives had been hit. Amongst many others that night, the Dunlop Rubber Works and Tunnel Road Cinema were damaged by high explosives.

We began to get used to the pattern of the attacks. The first would come in the early evening and then there would be a few hours break before the siren went again, summoning us back to the shelter until the early hours of the morning, sometimes until dawn.

On the night of 5th September, a very bad raid almost destroyed Liverpool Cathedral, damaging the beautiful stained glass windows and affecting much of the superstructure. High explosives were dropped over the whole of the City and we were much shaken when one exploded uncomfortably near to us in Claudia Street. As daylight was fading the next day the raiders returned. A large fire at a greaseworks lit up the sky but, thankfully, the raid did not last too long.

Over the next fortnight, we were summoned to the shelter on numerous occasions. Heavy Ack-Ack barrage thundered around us, a large number of incendiaries were dropped and, one night, intermittent raids covered a period of nearly ten hours.

The night before my eighth birthday, we suffered one of the severest raids yet. Twice during the day the sirens had sounded and, yet again, they came in the evening. The most horrific aspect of this particular raid was the report that firemen, trying to rescue people trapped in their houses, had been subjected to a terrifying machine gun attack by low flying planes.

Over the next six days we had more day and night raids. The underground railway was hit by a high explosive bomb and large fires raged in the dockland area.

When the sirens went during school hours, we made our way down to the cellar. The older children took the 'babies', the four and five year olds, on their knees and we were all anxious to have this honour. It was extraordinary how, even small children of seven, eight and nine years quickly became the comforters to the even smaller ones as the need arose. We cuddled, soothed and played with the tinies in much the same way as our own mothers did with us during the night raids.

Our teachers encouraged us to sing at the top of our voices and we had competitions to see which side of the cellar could sing the loudest. All cleverly designed to help block out the noise outside. We didn't mind, we sang and thoroughly enjoyed it. Some devious minds even dared to voice the opinion that it was 'better than having to do rotten old sums'. Children tend to live very much for the moment and we were happy enough to enjoy ourselves without bothering what the night might bring.

Our fighter planes and Ack-Ack barrage were doing us proud, had we but known it at the time. The enemy was finding it difficult to penetrate our defences without heavy losses. Towards the end of September, they began to devise a hit and run method of attack, whereby a lone plane left the main formation and, with engines silent, glided in, made its attack and then departed. As a result of this, much damage was done to the shops in the centre of the City, Parker Street, Clayton Square and Church Street.

Liverpool had its 121st raid on the night of 25th September, and two nights later the heaviest formation of bombers to date descended upon us with the most severe raid yet.

During that day, I had asked if I could prepare a 'Tuck Box' to take down to the shelter and began to fill a small cardboard box with all the goodies I could find. I kept this in readiness for the evening and, when the sirens sounded and we took cover as usual, my box went into the shelter with me.

We settled down as best we could, but the raid got heavier and heavier. The noise outside was deafening as one explosion after another rent the air. Suddenly my father leapt up and dashed up the stairs. Mother and I looked at each other in amazement wondering what on earth was the matter with him. We heard him taking the stairs two at a time and then, almost immediately, he was shouting "Sand, more sand, quickly".

Mother jumped up "Stay where you are and don't move" she ordered, grabbing a bucket of sand and rushing off to join my father.

I sat still listening to the dreadful noise all around me. Footsteps in the street running to and fro, men shouting to each other over each loud and successive explosion that made the very walls around me shake. A loud hammering beat on our front door.

"Open up, come on, we're all in this together" the men were shouting.

I heard the bolt being drawn back and the sound of heavy footsteps above me. Amidst the cocophony of noise upstairs, single footsteps came down the cellar stairs and a strange man appeared before me.

"Are you all on your own love?" he asked gently.

I nodded.

"Come on, I'll take you to my missus, she'll look after you" and with that he swept me up into his arms and carried me up the cellar stairs, still in my pyjamas and barefoot.

The living room was full of strangers as we went through and out the back door. In the street, the stranger covered my head with his coat but I managed to wriggle out. As I looked around it seemed to me as though the whole place was on fire. Flames from all the surrounding buildings licked greedily towards the sky which was itself alight with searchlights criss-crossed in every direction. The throbbing of planes overhead mingled with the noise of the Ack-Ack guns and explosions from bombs dropping near us. My 'rescuer' picked his way across Frodsham Street, for the road was strewn with hose pipes and rubble, and we made our way down City Road. I had no idea where he was taking me as, on and on he ran, but suddenly he turned into one of the side roads and stopped at a shelter.

"Will somebody take this kiddy?" he called.

I found myself being handed into the shelter and received by willing hands.

"Come on love, you're safe here with us" one of the women said as she put me down.

"Jimmy, shove up and make room for this little girl"

Jimmy shoved up and I sat down beside him. The shelter was full of women and children, all strangers to me.

"What's your name love?" someone asked in a very matter of fact voice. This was no time for making a fuss. They had no idea why I had been taken there and, provided everyone behaved as though it was a normal occurrence, there was less liklihood of my getting upset.

"Beryl" I whispered.

"Come on, pass those biscuits down here and give one to Beryl"

The biscuits found their way down to me but I was not hungry. By now I was convinced both my parents had been killed and that was why I had been taken out. A sudden crash made us all jump.

"Here, come on, why have you lot stopped singing?" a woman asked.

"Come on now, as loud as you can and with a bit of luck, that lot up there might hear you. 'Run Hitler, run Hitler, run, run, run . . .' "

Obviously my entry had, for the moment, caused the singing to stop but now everyone was in good voice again as they belted out the well known parody to the tune of "Run Rabbit Run"

What I did not know was that, whilst I was being 'rescued', my parents and many willing helpers were frantically trying to extinguish the fire in our bathroom which had been caused by an incendiary bomb. My father had recognised the 'swish' as it fell and that was what had sent him scuttling upstairs so quickly before the fire got a hold. As soon as my mother had an opportunity she came to the cellar stairs.

"Are you alright?" she called to me.

When she got no answer she flew down the stairs to see what I was doing and found the place empty. Panic stricken, she assumed I had run out into the street on my own. Unfortunately my 'rescuer' had not thought to tell my parents that he had taken me to his wife.

As far as my mother was concerned, the house could burn down once she discovered I was missing. Her main concern now was to find me so, leaving my father and the other men to fight the fire, she and a neighbour set about looking for me. They searched every street calling in all the shelters to see if I was there until, finally, they came upon the right one. Thankfully mother hugged me and I her. Now I believed it was my father who had been killed but mother did her best to reassure me he was safe and promised he would come and see me as soon as he had the opportunity.

"Will you ask him to bring my tuck box?" I asked.

Later, my father came down, with the tuck box and I was reassured. I stayed in the shelter with those kind people until the 'All Clear' went and it was safe to return home.

Back home all was chaos. Our next door neighbours came in to see the damage but I refused to go upstairs at all. I was scared in case the bomb went off again. I found it hard to believe it was now harmless. No sooner had they come back downstairs than we heard loud shouting in the street.

"Get back in the shelters" the wardens were yelling at the top of their voices "the raids still on, the all clear was a mistake".

Everyone scattered to their own shelters as quickly as possible and it was several hours before we were able to return to our beds.

No more tuck boxes for me. Mother said she thought I must have had a premonition that something dreadful was going to happen that night, for never before had I ever thought of making up a tuck box and, needless to say, I never did again.

Next morning I was only too eager to go and view the damage for myself. By now I was certain that the bomb was safe and, what was more important, I wanted the 'fin'. We children collected shrapnel avidly and there was much competition as to who had the best collection. We kept our shrapnel in small boxes and took it to school where we swopped bits and pieces with each other. No-one so far had managed to get the fin off a bomb. Bits and pieces of assorted metal yes, but a fin off a real bomb, that was something else and I knew only too well that it would cause something of a stir when I walked in. My parents agreed that I could have it so, carefully extracting it from the wreckage, I tucked it safely away in my box.

Later, I tripped off to school proudly carrying my box of shrapnel with the 'fin' taking pride of place. I soon had an eager group of children around me and got many offers of 'swops' but there was no way I was going to swop my precious 'fin'. Even our teacher was interested to see my souvenir and hear how I had come by it and she soon found herself being overwhelmed with questions about the type of bomb it had originated from.

Our house was not the only one to have an incendiary bomb dropped on it that night, for they had come down like rain from the skies. A string of them had fallen in the City Road area. Among the many that fell near to us, one managed to land in the old Billiard Hall opposite and, as this was now being used as a paper warehouse, the whole place had gone up like dry tinder. Another fell on a house in Luxmore Road and the fire had been so fierce that the property had been almost gutted to the ground. No wonder it had seemed to me that the whole place was on fire — it was.

In the City that night, 1,000 Income Tax forms were destroyed by fire — no doubt there was some secret rejoicing over that — whilst over the water in Birkenhead, the old Argyle Theatre was virtually destroyed and, with it, a history of Theatre.

The following night we had three raids in quick succession, whilst the next day nine Hurricanes saved us from a serious daylight attack when they spotted nine Heinkel III bombers heading for Liverpool and managed to chase them off. Later that night we were back in the shelter again, for six long hours, whilst yet another incendiary attack rained down on Merseyside.

By now we had very few windows left in our house and most of the surrounding houses and shops were all in the same state. Our bathroom was a total wreck with the woodwork and walls badly burnt and blackened from the fire that had raged through it.

Some of the local shops had lost their big plate glass windows and began to serve customers through the window rather than over the counter. This tempted a few local lads to try their hands at a little amateurish looting by helping themselves to tins out of the Co-op window. After a few sharp clips around the ear from passers-by they quickly turned to more honourable activities. The local butcher, still lucky enough to have his window intact, decided to give us all a smile and chalked across it in big white letters "BECAUSE OF HITLER, THE PORTIONS ARE LITTLER".

October came and brought with it more air-raids. Rumour was rife, mainly because it was difficult to find out what has happening in other areas due to censorship. We did, however, hear of a frightening experience when a bus conductor in Liverpool thought he saw a plane flying very low. A few minutes later, he heard the clatter of the Ack-Ack guns and, looking back, was horrified to see the same plane drop even lower and fly towards them. As the first splutter of machine gun fire spat out from the plane the driver, with great presence of mind, swerved to the opposite side of the road and missed the gunfire completely. Thankfully; no damage was done and there were no casualties, save for an auxiliary fireman who had his hat knocked off, presumably by a bullet.

After this, Merseyside had a brief respite as Hitler deserted us for a whole week. During this time we took a deep breath, had a few good nights sleep and assessed the damage so far.

To date, the Cathedral had suffered much damage, as had many other smaller churches including Mossley Hill Church, St. Margaret's, Anfield, St. Cuthbert's, Everton and the Hamlet Free Church. Several hospitals and nursing homes had been hit, the Ice Rink and a Football Ground, a High School in Aigburth, a Cinema, the Docks and all the area around, the City centre including many of the large stores and so many, many ordinary homes so numerous they could not be counted.

On the night of 7th October, it began again. In order to try and avoid our fighter planes the early evening raids were discarded in favour of a later attack when the bombers descended upon us in a succession of small waves or as single machines.

The following afternoon, one of our customers was at the Pier Head. She came into the shop later and told us how she and hundreds of others, watched a brief but fierce battle over Eastham Locks. We found out later that a British pilot and two Czech airmen had brought down a Junkers 88 in flames. A few days later, after more night raids during which South John Street, Paradise Street and Hanover Street got the worst of it, another vicious dog fight took place in the early part of the evening when three German Dorniers attempted to attack Liverpool and all three were shot down by our fighter planes. Later that night another raid took place, during which both high explosives and incendiary bombs were dropped.

By now the bombers were used to the Ack-Ack barrage awaiting them around the City and tried another approach. Circling round and round the fringe of the guns, individual planes darted in, made their attack and flew out again. It was almost as though they were playing Cowboys and Indians.

The next evening, more than forty bombers attacked Liverpool and some of the heaviest Ack-Ack gunfire resounded over the City as shrapnel showered down.

During the whole of this time, we were very concious of the black-out. The least little chink of light could be seen from the sky, so we were told, and the wardens were vigilant in their watch for any black-out irregularities. The slightest sign of a light and they would hammer long and hard on the door shouting "Put that light out!"

It was pitch black in our back yard, and one evening my mother, after having finished the washing up, went to deposit some rubbish in the bin at the bottom of the yard. Suddenly, we heard her cry out and both my father and I rushed out. Mother was holding her hands over her face and blood was streaming down her cheeks. She had walked into the wall, broken her glasses and the glass had cut into her cheek. My father helped her inside and tended to her cuts, whilst I fussed around anxious to reassure myself that she was alright.

It seemed there were many dangers around us at that time, for there were many reports of accidents in the black-out as people could not see where they were going. Not only had we to be aware of the danger from the skies above, we also had to be aware of the dangers on the ground below.

CHAPTER 8

"Hurry, The Purple Light's On"

8

After the recent heavy raids and, more particularly, the incendiary bomb attack during which our house received a direct hit, we had hardly any windows left. In addition, quite a considerable amount of structural damage had been done, not to mention a large hole in the roof where the bomb had come through. All the window frames were loose and some hung out with a gap of several inches between them and the walls. There was little chance of anything being done to rectify the situation for some time yet and nearly all the other houses in our area were in the same condition.

We were lucky, we still had a house, for many did not and could only look down at the pile of bricks and rubble that had once been their home. For those people, the authorities set up Rest Centres, where they could stay together as a family whilst alternative accommodation was sought. Not an easy matter in a City where dozens were being made homeless every night. The Womens Voluntary Service gave food and comfort to the homeless and often were on hand to supply a much needed cup of tea whilst the bombs were still falling around them.

There did not seem to be much prospect of a lull in the bombing, so my parents made arrangements for us to go and stay with my mother's sister and her family who lived in Upper Warwick Street, Princes Park. This was a short term arrangement until our own house was made liveable again.

Each evening, mother and I would leave home about six o'clock and get the No. 25 tram, whilst my father stayed on to close the shop and follow up later with Billy, our dog. This worked quite well as my aunty and uncle had a large cellar and there was ample room for us all. By now we automatically went to bed in the cellar or shelter, for it was only a waste of time going upstairs.

Most evenings we would have our meal before leaving home, spend the night at Upper Warwick Street and return home to City Road the following morning. Our first job on returning home was to sweep up the broken glass and debris left from the previous night's bombing.

The local warden knew we were making this journey and always called in to warn us if the 'purple light' was on — this meant enemy raiders had been sighted. Once we knew 'they' were on their way, it was time for us to be on our way.

One evening my father arrived alone. I saw him talking to my mother and they both seemed very worried about something.

"Where's Billy?" I asked.

"He's with Mrs. Close" my father told me. Mrs. Close was our next door neighbour and, although we knew her well and were good friends, it seemed rather odd to me that my father should leave Billy with her rather than bring him along as usual. We were already in the shelter as the siren had gone early that night and, with everyone else busy chattering away, I found it difficult to pursue the matter of why my father had not brought Billy.

Next morning mother wouldn't hear of me going home and insisted that I stay at my aunt's. I was sure now that something was wrong. I knew better than to argue for it never got me anywhere so I just had to stay put. Later that evening, when my parents arrived together, there was still no Billy.

"Why haven't you brought Billy? Where is he?"

Mother came and put her arm round me and said, "Billy's gone to heaven" explaining that Billy was a very old dog and had had a good life but now, sadly, it was over and time for him to have a good rest.

I wept sad tears for Billy. He had been a faithful old dog and, although my parents had had him long before I was born, he'd never shown any signs of jealousy towards me but rather taken upon himself the job of guard — wherever I went Billy went.

How much more bitter those tears would have been had I then known what really happened to Billy. My parents told me the true story many years later.

Apparently after mother and I had left, my father had gone to the door to bring in the newspaper rack when, suddenly, a plane appeared low in the sky. A warden yelled "Get down, it's a Jerry" and everybody scuttled to take cover as fast as they could. As my father turned, he tripped and fell on top of Billy who had been following behind. To his horror my father found Billy couldn't move, his ribs had been broken. Unable to summon a vet at that time of night and unable to bring Billy to my aunties, father made him as comfortable as possible and then, reluctantly had to leave him. Next morning, Mrs. Close told my father that Billy had howled piteously all night. My father decided there and then that he would suffer no more and the vet was called immediately.

Although we were sad at the loss of Billy, many families were mourning even greater losses as the raids got heavier and heavier. On the night of 17th October, the West Wing of Fazakerley Sanatorium was completely demolished. The next night, a four hour long raid resulted in the water mains on Aigburth Road being hit and a vast amount of damage in Priory Road. On 23rd October, Merseyside had its 200th air raid.

I spent the next few days at my auntie's as my parents thought it would help to take my mind off losing Billy. My cousin had several friends who lived near and I was soon playing happily again.

We often played in Thackeray Street and one day, as we stood in a group talking, some other boys from nearby started calling. I had no idea who these strange boys were, although the others seemed to know them well enough. A somewhat menacing atmosphere began to develop as, after some name calling, the boys began to square up in readiness for a fight. We girls waited in the background anxiously when, suddenly, the other gang backed off and began to run towards an entry further up the street. We followed and clustered around the opening to see where they had gone. There was a shout of "Look out!" and everyone ducked except me. One of the gang had picked up a brick and flung it at us. I felt a sharp stab of pain in my lip and my mouth seemed to go numb. As I raised my hand to my face, I felt the hot trickle of blood running through my fingers. The others stood staring at me, stunned for a moment by what had happened and then, suddenly, they sprang into action. My cousin and the other boys shot off down the entry after the boy who had thrown the brick, whilst the girls crowded around me offering comfort. When they realised how bad the cut was they took me home to my aunt.

After several attempts to stop the bleeding my auntie realised it was going to need professional attention. Giving me a large handkerchief to hold over my mouth, we set off for the local Chemist only to find it was half-day closing. Off we trooped up Upper Warwick Street towards the Doctors. Auntie, suddenly realising we had a little procession following us, quickly despatched them off to their various homes.

As we approached Princes Road we saw my mother coming towards us.

"What on earth have you done?" she cried.

Explanations were given as we carried on walking. As soon as we arrived at the Doctors we were shown immediately into the Surgery. It smelt horribly of antiseptic and I was none too happy about it at all. The Doctor, a tall dark man, eyed me up and down.

"Come here and let's have a look at you" he said, placing me firmly between his knees.

"It's going to need several stitches I'm afraid" he announced getting to his feet and walking over to a small cabinet from where he began to collect various items of equipment.

"Now stand still and don't move" he instructed as he placed me firmly back between his knees.

I stood still until the needle pierced my lip and then quickly pulled away with a yelp of pain.

"That's no good, no good at all young lady" he said pulling me back, "You must stay perfectly still."

Once more he tried and once more I yelped and pulled away from him.

"It's absolutely no use like this, I'll have to give her gas" he said irritably.

I couldn't believe my ears. Gas! He couldn't! He wouldn't!!!

To my horror I found myself being lifted onto a large couch and neither my mother nor my auntie made any attempt to stop this. In fact, they were helping him!! I struggled and wriggled for all my worth but the Doctor held on.

"Hold her tight while I get the mask over her face" he ordered.

I struggled all the more. He was not going to give me gas, I didn't want to die yet. I fought with all my strength. As far as I was concerned I was literally fighting for my life and fear gave me extra strength.

Recently, a whole family had been gassed in their cellar during a particularly bad raid and I was convinced that it was the same type of gas. I didn't know there were different types and this was merely an anaesthetic.

The Doctor got more and more annoyed as I struggled.

"This is disgraceful" he said angrily "I can't possibly treat her like this".

By now I was past caring and wept bitterly, not only from the pain in my lip but from the sheer terror of thinking he was trying to kill me. If only he had taken the trouble to explain what he was trying to do and reassure me about the type of gas he was intending to use.

Eventually the Doctor strapped my lip up firmly with sticking plaster, warned my mother that I would be disfigured for life as the lip would develop into a 'hare' lip as it healed and told me it was my own fault for being such a naughty girl. As he escorted us to the door he could not resist a finale gibe "I've got a little girl of my own and I hope she turns out to be a lot braver than you" was his parting shot.

As soon as we got back to my aunties, the first thing to do was put the kettle on. Everybody felt badly in need of a cup of tea. Unfortunately, I found I couldn't drink from a cup but the problem was soon solved with a packet of drinking straws which, although quickly disintegrating in the hot tea, stood me in good stead until a special beaker could be purchased from the Chemist the following day.

When my lip finally healed, it left hardly any scar at all, let alone the disfiguration threatened by the Doctor. In actual fact, the scar is even smaller than it would have been had stitches been inserted.

"Are you going to Princes Park tonight?" the local warden asked, popping his head round the shop door.

"Yes, why? Is something the matter?" asked my mother.

"Get off as quick as you can, the purple light's on" he warned.

There was no time to be lost now. Mother and I got ready and my father told us to get off and he would follow on his bicycle as soon as he'd locked up.

As the tram began its shaky, jerky journey across the City, we hoped and prayed we would all get there safely before the siren went. As we approached Netherfield Road the familiar wailing started.

"Right, that's it, we can't go any further. Everybody off" announced our driver.

"Just a minute, you can't order us off like that. You have to take us to a public shelter" I was amazed to hear my mother saying.

"That's right, that's right" the other passengers joined in "there's no shelter here".

The driver looked around and, realising his passengers were not going to leave, somewhat reluctantly agreed to carry on. Thankfully, we all sat down again and with a jerk and a shudder, the tram began to move once more.

"There, that's Rupert Hill up there and there's a shelter over there. I'm going no further" the driver announced after we had travelled a short way.

We peered into the darkness. "I suppose that'll have to do" mother conceded.

The wardens were soon directing us to a large street shelter and we all went inside and sat down on the long benches. By now the guns were going fiercely and the drone of planes getting heavier and heavier. Someone outside the shelter shouted to indicate they wanted to come inside. The light had to be extinguished whilst the door was opened. As soon as the light went on again we looked up to see a large stout woman in the garb of a "Mary Ellen".

"Jeez, what a night" she gasped pulling a large black shawl closely around her shoulders. "I don't know where me old fella is and that's a fact. Last I saw of him, he was going down the pub. Knowing him he's probably had that many he doesn't even know there's a raid on!"

She re-adjusted the shawl, made to sit down and then, suddenly, changed her mind and turned towards the door.

"Oh gawd, I've just remembered" she wailed, holding a podgy hand to her forehead "I've left a pan of scouse on the stove".

We all saw the funny side of this.

"Hey Mr. Warden" she yelled through the closed door "If you're going anywhere near the top of the hill, do us a favour and pop in our 'ouse and turn me scouse off will yer"

The raid was now at its height. Explosion after explosion rent the air and the walls of the shelter shuddered with each successive bang. The light in the centre swung from side to side as though the very earth itself was moving. We crouched together on the benches as the scream of bombs and the thunder of explosions echoed all around us.

"I'll have to wash me steps again tomorrow after all this" Mary Ellen observed. "He's a mucky begger that 'Itler, he don't 'alf make a mess of 'em with all this. If ever I get 'old of 'im I'll give 'im a bucket of water and he can clean the lot in our street!"

We laughed as her comment relieved, for a moment, the fear we all shared.

Just then, one of the wardens stormed angrily into the shelter yelling "Whose left a tram on top of the hill?"

Our driver stood up.

"Well, go and switch your bloody lights off, we're a sitting target here, they're bombing all round it".

Red faced with embarrassment, our driver scuttled out to switch off the offending lights whilst a gasp of horror went round the shelter. We knew only too well how dangerous even a small light was, the tram lights must have looked like a veritable lighthouse from above. The warden went out muttering some very uncomplimentary things about tram drivers whilst we sat awaiting the worst. By now everyone in the shelter was getting to know each other. Our usual English reserve had gone, we were united in our predicament and we tried to cheer each other up. Mary Ellen talked to everyone and had the whole place laughing and singing with her. She was one of the good old Liverpool 'characters'.

After an hour or so, things began to get a little quieter and we wondered if we dare make an attempt to move on before the next wave of bombers descended upon us. Our driver stood up.

"If anyone wants to chance it, I'll go on a bit further, but if it comes on heavy again we'll have to stop and take our chance in the nearest shelter"

We agreed to chance it and trooped out after him into the darkness and back on to the tram.

I sat near the window as we made our way along the road again. The searchlights still lit up the sky but there was, as yet, no drone of aeroplanes. The first wave, having dropped their bombs and done their worst, were on their way home. The second wave had not yet reached us. We could see the damage that had been done so far as we passed by roads with many houses reduced to piles of rubble. In some places, the rescue workers were still digging frantically in their attempts to free people. Ambulances stood ready and waiting.

"I don't think I can go any further" our driver called out.

We peered out to see what was the matter, and the driver climbed down and walked ahead. We could just make him out talking to some other men. A few minutes later he was back.

"It's alright, we'll make it. There's a hole in the road where a bomb dropped, but it's not all that big and its just missed the track so we'll be able to get round it" he explained. We were off again.

About ten minutes later, whilst looking out of the window, I could scarcely believe my eyes when a very familiar figure rode past on a bicycle.

"Mummy, there's daddy" I shouted.

"Where?" Mother peered through the window to where I was pointing but he had gone, disappeared into the darkness.

"Are you sure it was Daddy?"

"Yes, yes. It was, it was."

"Well, we can't do very much about it now. I suppose he's come to look for us. They must all be wondering where on earth we've got to" she said worriedly.

We finished the journey without further incident.

"Where on earth have you been? George has been out twice to look for you" Auntie greeted us.

Mother explained what had happened and just then my father rode up on his bike.

We were alright now. We were all together again.

CHAPTER 9

"The Christmas Raids"

9

We stayed at my aunties for several weeks and then, when the windows had been boarded up and the house made reasonably habitable again, we went home. City Road looked very war torn with few windows still in existence, much of the brickwork pitted from shrapnel and many of the houses in the side streets damaged.

At the far end of City Road was the 'Brew', as we called it. This was, in fact, a bridge over the main railway line to the Docks that was used for carrying goods and munitions. German intelligence sources were obviously only too well aware of this vital supply link, for they made repeated attempts to try and put it out of action. The surrounding area was bombed time and time again but they failed to hit their target, the railway line.

One Saturday morning I was busy sweeping up the pavement.

"Trying to make the road a bit wider then?" a customer smiled as she opened the shop door on her way to 'pay the papers'. "You can come and do mine when you've finished".

I declined the offer to brush her pavement as politely as possible. The comment about 'making the road wider' I didn't understand, and secretly put it down to one of those stupid remarks grown-ups seem to like to make.

A plane suddenly swept down from behind the clouds and I glanced up. As I watched, it came lower and lower until it seemed to me that it was almost ready to land. This I had to tell my father, and promptly dropped the brush and dashed into the shop.

"Daddy, daddy, quick, come and see. There's a plane coming down, it looks as if it's going to land"

The two customers in the shop joined in the rush to get out and see but, as soon as my father took a look, he shoved us all back into the shop shouting "Get down! Get down! It's a Jerry!"

No siren had sounded and, fortunately, there was no incident of any kind, so we assumed that it must have been a reconnaissance plane taking photographs. Of course, due to security reasons, no official mention was ever made of the plane, so we never really found out just what it was doing.

This lack of communiction was a very sore point on Merseyside. We realised that it was a major port handling troop movements and goods, but surely the Germans knew only too well how hard they had bombed Liverpool.

"I don't know why they never mention us" complained a large woman who was having a free read of the front page of the Echo whilst waiting to be served.

"Look at this, 'A North West town suffered great damage last night' " she read aloud. "We don't have to be told which North West town do we and I'll bet the Jerries know which one, so why can't they just come out with it and say 'Liverpool'? "

"You can't even find out what's happening on the other side of town" another woman commented.

"Oh I know" agreed the first, folding the Echo and putting it back on the counter, "my sister lives up Clubmoor and you try finding out what's going on there"

Little news of the Merseyside bombing was ever printed due to security reasons. The 'Liverpool Echo' ran an article saying 'We have the right to know' but the authorities decided otherwise and it was not until much, much later that the full extent of Merseyside's bombardment became known.

The King and Queen paid a visit to the bombed areas of Bootle, Liverpool, Birkenhead and Wallasey and most people felt that this was, at least, some small recognition of all we had been suffering.

November went out with one of the heaviest raids we had yet experienced. The sirens sounded at 7.23 p.m. and explosives and incendiaries rained down over the City. The main weight of the attack took place in the first two and a half hours until 10.00 p.m. and during that time, two hundred people were killed. It was not until 4.00 a.m. that the raiders finally left our skies and headed for home, leaving Liverpool to pick itself up and prepare for work the next day.

Little did we know, but that night we were in for another shock. Someone had had the bright idea of adding an extra dimension to our defences in the form of a 'mobile gun'. This was merely an Ack-Ack gun placed on the back of a lorry which then careered around the streets firing as it went. Unfortunately, no-one thought to warn the unsuspecting population in the areas in which it operated and, the first night it went into action, it caused almost more consternation than the actual raid itself.

As the planes drew near, our new defence weapon went tearing along the roads at full speed, firing merrily as it hurtled round and round the corners like some demented elephant on the rampage. The vibration it caused as it bolted along set every door knocker and letter-box banging whilst the occupants of the houses, sitting down in the shelters, wondered what on earth was going on.

Heads began popping out, not very prudently it must be said. Neighbours looked wide-eyed with astonishment at each other.

"What the hell's that?" they shouted as the monster, spitting fire, skidded round yet another corner.

"Get back, get back" yelled the frantic wardens. We were more interested in the monster.

Round and round it scudded. "What on earth is it?" asked one man as, yet again it disappeared from view leaving all the door knockers banging in its wake.

"It's a mobile gun" one of the warden's finally informed us.

"Mobile gun! Mobile gun. . . . " an elderly man spluttered "it's a bloody mobile monstrosity".

There were no prizes for guessing the main topic of conversation in the shelters that night.

We were still spending most nights in the shelter, but the daily routine continued as near normal as possible. Factory and office workers made their way to work as usual although some found, on arrival, that their place of employment had been destroyed in the night. It was not unusual to see some firms trying to conduct their business in the street beside the pile of rubble that, until the previous evening, had been their offices. Many files and papers and much office equipment had been destroyed but, somehow or other, they managed to carry on as best they could.

The sense of humour of Liverpool people prevailed throughout the blitz and was evident in many ways. In front of one building, almost demolished by a bomb, stood a notice "These premises are for sale in part or whole". Some unknown wag crossed out the 'w' leaving the notice to read "These premises are for sale in part or hole".

We were now being exhorted to save as much as possible and thousands of small National Savings Groups sprang up throughout the country. Our school had its own group and each morning, after the Register had been called, our teacher would collect the savings money and issue us with stamps of equivalent value which we then stuck into a book and converted into Savings Certificates once we had acquired the necessary amount.

"Can I run a Savings Group?" I asked my mother.

"It'd be a lot of work, you'd have to do it properly, no messing about" she said.

"I would, honestly I would" I assured her.

"I don't know whether they'll let you at your age, but you can see what they say".

Mother helped me write a letter of application and I was more than delighted when the authorities registered my application, giving me the number 99/1/3960. I received a supply of savings books, forms, a rubber date stamp and ink pad and felt very important indeed. I went along to the Post Office in City Road, bought some stamps and I was in business.

I sold stamps to my friends and my parents allowed me to set up a little corner in the shop to sell stamps to our customers. I had always loved the old Post Office sets which came along in the form of Christmas presents but this was even better, this was the real thing, not a toy.

The following Saturday my father took me into town, whilst mother looked after the shop. A real Messerschmitt was on display on St. George's Plateau and was, in fact, one that had been shot down over Merseyside. There was a huge queue waiting to file past the plane and we joined on the end. It was a strange feeling coming so near to an enemy plane and the sight of the black cross on the wings sent shivers down my spine. The plane was part of a big display organised in Liverpool for a War Weapons Drive to encourage even more saving.

At school we girls were now busy knitting 'comforts for the Forces'. Those of us who had a relative already in the Forces would knit for them whilst the rest produced balaclava helmets, mittens and other garments which were sent, en masse, to the authorities for distribution amongst the troops in general.

My cousin was in the Royal Navy so I decided to knit a scarf for him. Mother got a pattern for me and, armed with some navy blue wool and a pair of needles, I was soon busy clicking away alongside the rest of the class. I was not a very fast knitter and got terribly impatient when the scarf seemingly refused to 'grow'. I pulled and tugged at it hoping to make it a bit longer and, every now and then, managed to persuade mother to help. She would knit a few inches and then it was back to the slow progress of my own efforts. It took me until 1944 to finish that scarf and, when it was completed, I felt enormously proud of my efforts but even more thankful that it was finally done.

Whilst we girls were busy with our knitting, the boys began digging up the small back garden at the rear of the school. They were 'Digging for Victory' and were busily engaged in preparing the soil in readiness for the Spring sowing. Radishes proved to be one of their earliest successes but cabbages, peas and beans soon followed in their wake and we looked forward with pleasure to their harvesting.

As December dawned upon us, thoughts of Christmas began coming to the fore but we all knew that this year it would be very different from those we had previously known. We hoped and prayed for a respite from the air raids, at least over the festive period, but as of yet there seemed little prospect of that happening for we were still in the midst of the blitz and it seemed to be getting even worse.

On 3rd December, we had an exceptionally heavy raid that brought great tragedy to our City. A surface shelter was hit and two people killed so the rest flocked down to a basement shelter underneath a school. Two tramcars had also stopped outside the school and the occupants of both trams had taken cover in the same shelter. Packed like sardines, most of the people had gone into the inner section. When the explosion came the lights went out, glass shattered down and the roof crashed in. Fire broke out in the boiler room and rescue workers dug frantically to release the trapped people. Sixty were brought out alive, but one hundred and eighty were killed. A special service was held later that week in Anfield Cemetery as the unidentified were buried in a mass grave. The Lord Mayor placed a wreath on behalf of the City of Liverpool and all sections of the community were represented at the service. It was one of the worst disasters Liverpool suffered.

Hardly had we recovered from this devastating blow when the City had its 300th raid on the night of 12th December. Earlier that day we had all sat wondering what on earth was going on when the earth seemed to shake beneath us, although no siren had sounded. This time we couldn't very well blame Hitler, it was an earth tremor centred on the North Wales area.

Christmas was now approaching rapidly. My mother had already made our Christmas Pudding but we were all a bit dubious as to what it was going to taste like. With the shortage of cooking fats she, like all the other housewives, had had to resort to using an ingenious recipe which had been published in the "Food Facts" column in the paper. The recipe had included carrots — good for helping you to see in the dark we were told — and liquid paraffin. This latter sometimes had rather unfortunate results.

Although we were eagerly looking forward to whatever Christmas presents we might get we were not at all pleased with the ones Hitler had planned for us in the shape of the infamous 'Christmas Raids'. On the nights of 20th, 21st and 22nd December, each raid seemed longer than the previous night. The siren went at 6.20 p.m. on the first night and the all clear did not sound until 4.00 a.m. next morning. Again the following night we were in the shelter from 6.38 p.m. until 5.15 a.m. next morning.

The toll of death and disaster as a result of these raids was not fully known until long, long after, but included a number of shelters being hit including a communal one. St. George's Hall, the Assize Courts, where hundreds of people were sheltering underneath, was in danger of collapsing and, at the very peak of the raid, they were taken out and moved to other-shelters. In Roe Street, a fire engine responding to a call disappeared into a crater killing its crew. Bootle, Litherland, Crosby, Birkenhead and Wallasey all suffered severely. The docks were alight with flames that licked high into the sky whilst a delayed action bomb burst the banks of the Leeds-Liverpool Canal. We needed no Christmas lights or Illuminations that year, for the City was lit up in a way that no-one had ever before, or ever again, wanted to see.

Food warehouses in Dublin Street and the Waterloo Grain House were on fire. Cunard Buildings and the Dock Board Offices were hit. A bomb penetrated between two underground shelters pinning most of the occupants against the roof — forty eight people were brought out alive, but, forty two were killed.

One of the worst incidents was in Bentinck Street, where five railway arches were serving as an unofficial shelter. This was crowded with people and received a direct hit causing the arches to collapse in huge concrete blocks. After many days of rescue work, forty two bodies were brought out. Hundreds of houses were hit, especially in the Anfield area, where a direct hit on a large shelter caused the worst single tragedy of the night when seventy two people lost their lives. On these three nights alone, 356 people were killed.

As Christmas Eve dawned, we wearily made our way back to our beds. The Liverpool Echo did not wish their readers the usual "Merry Christmas and Happy New Year" but chose to echo the sentiments of all its readers in the fervent hope for "A Peaceful Christmas".

Mother got out our old box of Christmas decorations, new ones were not available that year. We dusted them down and hung them around the living room. The old artificial tree was brought out into service once again and the living room began to look cheerful and christmassy.

Now, the problem was how to cook the Christmas Dinner. Most of us had no gas supply whatsoever, the mains having been fractured during the bombing. Mother had managed to acquire a small duck and one of our neighbours, Mrs. Malone, offered to cook it in her 'kitchen oven'. All around us arrangements for communal cooking were being made as those fortunate enough to have old fashioned kitchen ovens took upon themselves the task of cooking for their less fortunate neighbours. Rotas were drawn up so that the food could be cooked in batches.

Christmas morning dawned and I fell eagerly upon my presents in the 'pillow case' at the bottom of the bed. It was sadly depleted this year, but we were grateful for what we could get. The excitement was still there as I ripped open the paper and scanned the contents.

As soon as the duck was prepared and put in a roasting dish, I was despatched off to Mrs. Malone in Emery Street to leave it with her for cooking. As I entered her kitchen, the aroma of delicious roast meat assailed my senses. She carefully opened the oven door and withdrew a roasting tin containing a brown and succulent chicken, not very large, but adequate for a good Christmas dinner for some family. This was followed by a tiny piece of pork and a small joint of lamb. Carefully she placed them on the table to await their owners and I watched as our duck was put on a shelf and the heavy black doors closed.

"About one and a half hours and it'll be done to a turn" she told me. My mouth started watering already in anticipation.

CHAPTER 10

"Terry's New Home"

10

Christmas was over, the New Year heralded in 1941 and Liverpool, along with the rest of the country, breathed again as the raids slackened off for a time. The Luftwaffe still paid some visits to Liverpool but, compared to their past efforts, these were of a minor nature. We began to relax a little and even ventured out to see "Mother Goose" at the Empire. It was about the only pantomime on in Liverpool as most of the theatres had been damaged and many of the entertainers were now busy with their ENSA commitments. Instead of staging their usual pantomime, the Royal Court chose to put on a Revue. We decided to stay traditional and opted for the pantomime.

During the Christmas holidays, I spent my time helping in the shop and playing in Ripon Street.

"Are you coming to my party?" Eileen asked me.

"Yes please"

"My mum'll give you a proper invitation"

True to her word, Eileen's mother presented me with an envelope containing the much prized invitation and, clutching it in my hot little hand, I ran off home.

"Mummy, mummy, I've been invited to a party" I informed her with great excitement.

On the big day, we all converged on the birthday girl's home, dressed in our best frocks and each bearing a small gift. After the usual party games of 'Pass the Parcel', 'Little Alexandra' and 'Oranges and Lemons' came the big moment — the Party Tea. We sat down to sandwiches, jelly and, best of all, iced buns. Icing sugar had been off the market for some time and we thought the icing was as good as caviar. Each bun had been carefully spread with chocolate icing and they tasted like nectar as we bit around the edges, trying to save the icing to last. One special bun had been kept aside and on this was placed a candle for the birthday girl to blow out whilst we all chorused "Happy Birthday" at the top of our voices. A couple of years ago and it would have been a large pink and white iced birthday cake but, with the rationing, this was now impossible. As children, we never for one moment thought of comparing this birthday spread to the ones of the past.

Occasionally, some of the local Churches would organise a party for the children who attended their Sunday Schools. The Methodist Church on County Road did just that and, as each child was allocated a table and could invite three or four friends, I found myself invited to attend.

We all contributed something towards the table, or at least our mothers did. Rations were carefully saved so that a few small cakes could be provided to help eke out the sandwiches and jellies. The jellies became the centrepieces and mothers, who had once prided themselves on their skills at cake decorating, now turned those same skills to making fancy jellies. Apart from the moulds which produced rabbits, fish and other shapes, we now saw some ingenious new designs. Jellies of different colours, chopped up, and arranged to resemble flowers, crowns, the rising sun and many other designs.

There was to be a silver collection and we all trotted off happily clutching our sixpences, shillings or, in some cases, tiny silver threepenny pieces, better known to us as 'threepenny joeys'.

Our parents seemed determined that we children suffered as little deprivation as possible and went out of their way to make things as happy as possible during the day. They could do nothing about the dreadful air-raids we had to endure night after night, neither did they have any control over the childish ailments that afflicted us war or no war. The most dreaded illness of all — diptheria — was still rife. Whenever a child complained of a sore throat, parents waited with dread in their hearts for the doctor to confirm or dispel their worst fears — was it diptheria. If it was diagnosed then it was off to the Isolation Hospital at Fazakerley. Some fortunate children recovered but many, many more, died before a vaccine was discovered which, thankfully, makes the disease a rarity today.

One morning I awoke feeling not at all well. My throat hurt, my jaws ached and I had a nasty headache. Mother scrutinised my face carefully.

"I think you've got mumps" she announced to my dismay.

I was confined to bed, the doctor was called and mother fetched an old woollen sock which she carefully spread with foul smelling goose grease, carefully hoarded in a screw top jar from the Christmas before last. This was then tied around my chin and fastened on top of my head like a pair of rabbits ears. I was most uncomfortable, the sock smelt horrible, it itched and made me feel hot and sticky but I had to bear with it.

It was not difficult to keep me entertained whilst in bed for I loved painting and crayoning. In addition mother moved an old gramophone to the side of the bed so that I could play the old records. Old some certainly were, with titles like "Why is the bacon so tough?" and "Have you any M-o-n-e-y?". There were, however, some newer ones as well and one of my favourites was "The White Cliffs of Dover". The gramophone had to be wound up with a big handle attached to the side and the needles required frequent changing but that was all part of the fun.

It had been snowing hard whilst I was confined to bed and the snow had come through the broken window frames. Mother had had a dreadful time mopping it up and trying to stuff the window frame with old cloths to prevent it coming through again.

"Just look at this" she said to the Doctor, pointing out the large gaps. "When are they going to do something about the bomb damage?"

It was not the ideal place to nurse a sick child but resources were strained to the limit and, although mother might complain, both she and the doctor knew that it would be a long time before any repairs could be done. It was hardly worth repairing something that might get damaged again the same night so we just had to make the best of it.

As soon as I had recovered I re-joined my mother in the shop. Supplies were short and, with less stock to sell, we now closed each afternoon re-opening in time for the evening papers. We still sold the old fashioned thick and thin twist much beloved by the older pipe smoking men who were very particular how their precious tobacco was cut. My parents had a special pair of scales kept solely for the purpose of weighing tobacco. These scales had a wooden base with two brass pans attached by a long brass pole and cross bar. Tiny weights of different value were added to one of the pans whilst the tobacco was placed in the other. When the two balanced perfectly you had the correct weight. A special tool was needed for cutting the tobacco and this consisted of a large wooden base with a knife attached by a hinge. The tobacco was placed on the wooden base and cut by means of pulling the knife down. With practice you could judge pretty accurately just how much tobacco would make up an ounce but it was never acceptable to the old gentlemen to have it cut in one piece, they always demanded a 'jockey'. This 'jockey', as they called it, was merely a tiny piece of tobacco cut separately from the main piece and added on to make up the weight.

My father was often late home from work as he had to take his turn on the fire-watching rota and, on these nights, mother and I would curl up in the big armchair in front of the fire, me on her knee, whilst she read one of my comics. My favourite story at that time was 'Sexton Blake and the Air-Raid Shelter Mysteries'.

The mystery was that all the street shelters in one neighbourhood were being systematically knocked down by large lorries as a gang of thieves searched for the jewels they had planted in the concrete of a half built shelter some time earlier. I loved it, but mother said later she'd thought it a stupid story when so many children had to spend so much of their time in shelters, just like the ones depicted in the story. Mother thought it would point out how vulnerable we were for, if a lorry could knock one down so easily, what would a bomb do! Of course that thought never occurred to me, I just took it for what it was, a jolly good exciting story. Childrens minds work differently from those of a grown-up.

Towards the end of January, our next door neighbour, Mrs. Close, came into the shop and I could see her busy whispering to my parents. Curious to know what was going on, I tried to listen in but could only hear a few snatched sentences that meant very little.

"Now don't bring him in otherwise we'll only fall for him" I heard mother say. Agog with curiosity I, of course, wanted to know who Mrs. Close wasn't to bring in and why would we fall for him.

"Never you mind, you shouldn't have been listening" was all I got.

Mrs. Close, wise in her years, took no notice and went off only to re-appear a few minutes later with the most adorable scottie dog I had ever seen. Gently, she set him down on the counter top.

"I thought I said don't bring him in" mother protested.

Mrs. Close just smiled, "Well, what do you think?" she asked.

I thought he was adorable. Suddenly I guessed what had been going on. Mrs. Close was trying to find a home for him.

"Can we have him?" I asked.

"I don't know, we'll have to see" mother said.

"Please, please say yes. Can we? Can we have him?" I begged running from one parent to another.

"Who'd look after him?" asked father.

"I would. I would. I'd look after him" I promised.

"You mean I would" mother corrected me.

"What do you think?" my father asked.

"Oh alright then" mother said.

I was overjoyed. I didn't know who to hug first, mother, father or the little dog.

"His name's Terry" Mrs. Close informed us.

"Well, don't you think you'd better take him in and let him see his new home then" father said.

I needed no second bidding and very soon Terry was cautiously sniffing around his new abode whilst I fussed over him like an old hen.

Mrs. Close, well pleased with her work, said "I'm glad that's settled. I knew you'd have him"

We had several raids during February and, once again, we were back in the shelter. Now I was happy to curl up in the big bed in the cellar with Terry at my side. I thought I was looking after him but I think it was probably the other way around for he gave me great consolation.

In March, a very heavy raid took place on Merseyside and this time the Luftwaffe concentrated mainly on Birkenhead and Wallasey. During this time the Birkenhead General Hospital had to be evacuated; a great number of fires were reported and Wallasey seemed to get the worst of all for the total number of deaths during that month was more than half the total for the whole nine months blitz period of 1940-41.

In general, the raids did seem to be easing off a bit so we began to go to the pictures again in the evening, usually on a Saturday night. If a raid commenced during the performance, a notice would be flashed on to the screen informing patrons that the sirens had sounded. There was no necessity to leave at this stage and it was only when the guns started firing that the final request would be made for patrons to leave the building and take cover in a shelter.

We were happily enjoying the picture one such evening when we were informed that the sirens had gone.

"Let's wait until the guns go" I said, anxious not to miss any of the picture.

Some ten minutes later, a notice came on the screen informing all patrons that the guns were now firing and we had to leave. We filed out and emerged onto Walton Road. Searchlights lit the sky and the guns were blazing away as we began walking home. A young couple were ahead of us. Suddenly the girl began to panic. Her boyfriend tried to console her but she was pleading to go into the first shelter they came to. Her panic began to communicate itself to me and I started crying.

"Now stop that and don't be silly, we'll soon be home" my father said in an attempt to calm me down.

"Please let's go in a shelter" I begged.

"Come, on we'll have a little run" my father said.

Both my parents took hold of me and we began to run. The young couple had now turned off to go into one of the street shelters and I wanted to follow them.

"We're nearly home, come on" urged my father.

On and on we ran. Down Walton Road, up Spellow Lane and soon we were in City Road and my father was getting his key out in readiness to open the door. By now the raid was coming on very heavy and I was more than relieved when we finally arrived on our own doorstep to be greeted by an ecstatic Terry. Once in our own shelter I looked around at my parents,

"We're alright now, aren't we. We're quite safe now we're in our own shelter".

Later my father said the shelter was worth its weight in gold if it had given me that sense of security.

April saw the end of our brief respite from the perpetual night raids for, on the night of 8th April, the sirens sounded at 8.17 p.m. and the all clear did not go until 3.45 a.m. next morning. That night there were about two hundred explosions on Merseyside. Incendiary bombs fell in the neighbourhood of Beaconsfield Road, fifty in Garston and two hundred in the Menlove Avenue district, whilst a large number also landed on the Lister Drive area of the City and the Electric Power Station. High explosives fell in the Edge Lane area demolishing a church and seriously damaging a Convent where twenty six nuns had a remarkable escape. Miraculously, there were no casualties from this raid. The enemy lost two planes, a night fighter got one which crashed between Southport and Lytham, whilst the second was blown to pieces in the air by Ack-Ack batteries south of the City.

The following night a small number of incendiaries were dropped and, again the next night, enemy planes were reported to have been in the area. On 16th April, another 'fire-raising' raid took place but although this lasted several hours there was little damage done and casualties were low. Only one fire lasted more than a half-hour and this was at a factory on the outskirts of the City.

The next four hours we had more raids and on 28th April, a Home for Babies and a suburban housing estate were victims of the indiscriminate bombing but, although casualties were comparatively few some, sadly, were fatal.

April was over and little did we know what the month of May was to bring.

CHAPTER 11

"The May Blitz"

11

The first day of May and the local children dressed up for the May processions. The little girls chose a May Queen and, proudly got up in a long frock with one of her mother's net curtains affixed to her head and a small bouquet of flowers clutched in her hot little hand, the small queen led her retinue up and down the street. This traditional ceremony was practised in many of the small side streets in Liverpool and symbolised the coming of Summer. Sadly, this year it also heralded in the beginning of the terrible and horrific May blitz when Hitler, despite his massive and horrendous blitzkrieg, found he could neither destroy the work of the Port of Liverpool nor break the spirit of the citizens who inhabited it.

On the first two nights we went to the shelter blissfully ignorant of what that week would bring. The raid was not too bad by previous standards as there were less than a hundred incidents in the area but the following night the scale of the raid doubled, although many of the enemy planes were successfully turned away by the Ack-Ack guns.

On the third night it seemed as if all hell had been let loose on Merseyside. It was difficult to differentiate between the gun fire and the swish of bombs whistling down and exploding as crash after crash almost deafened us. I cuddled Terry closer to me and mother and father listened anxiously as each explosion seemed to get nearer and nearer. There was no playing cards tonight. The heavy drone of planes overhead answered my unspoken question of "Are they overhead?" There was no doubt that tonight was going to be very bad indeed. Occasionaly, there would be a slight pause when everything seemed to go still and quiet and these moments were the worst, as we waited for the deafening explosion that would follow.

During one of these eerie, unnatural silences, we heard the sound of heavy footsteps in the street above and then the sound of voices shouting to each other.

"It's coming down on a parachute. It's going to be Ripon Street"

Silence again as those in the street watched with horror as a huge land mine descended slowly towards them on a parachute. My mother looked across anxiously as I clutched hold of her with one hand and held Terry tight with the other.

More running footsteps and shouting.

"The wind's got it, it's going further away. It's Index Street"

The waiting was almost unbearable and seemed like hours although, in reality, it was only minutes. Suddenly, the most terrible explosion rent the air. I buried my head in my mother's shoulder as we heard the sound of glass shattering down and the whole house shook above us.

"I'll go and see if they want any help" my father said.

"Tell them they can bring anyone they want in here" mother said.

After a while he came back looking very grave.

"It's Index Street and Arnot Street"

"Is it very bad?" mother asked.

My father shook his head slowly. "There's nothing anyone can do. The rescue workers are all down there now"

We sat numbed as the raid continued and then another terrific explosion, not unlike the previous one, sent us reeling once more.

"It's alright love, it's alright" my father soothed, as I made a grab for him.

On and on the raid continued all that dreadful, horrific night until finally, in the early hours of the morning, the all-clear finally sounded.

Next morning the devastation was horrifying. Almost three streets, Arnot, Index and Lowell had been destroyed by one bomb. The other land mine had fallen in Anfield Cemetery causing a huge crater. I didn't go to school that day, nor did many of the other children, and as I followed my mother around the shop our customers all had their own tales to tell of the previous night. I kept getting sent in to turn off the kettle only to find it had never been put on in the first place. Do all mothers have a convenient kettle that requires turning off just when the conversation is becoming interesting?

Naturally, I wanted to go out and play, but before I went Mother made me promise faithfully not to go anywhere near Index Street. The bottom of Ripon Street was as far as I was allowed and on no account was I to stray into Goodison Road.

As soon as I joined my friends, we began to discuss the events of the previous night just as the grown ups were doing and I found I was not the only one to have been forbidden access to the area in which the land mine had fallen.

"I'm not allowed to go any further than the bottom of the street" I announced.

"Neither am I"

"I know why we can't go" volunteered one knowledgeable soul.

"Why?" we all demanded.

" 'cos there's still legs and arms dangling from the lamposts" came the grisly reply.

We were all keen to put our spoke in now.

"Did you hear about the two old women who kept all their money in a box and when the bomb fell, it blew open and they're still trying to pick up the pounds notes?"

"What about the one that fell in the cemetery?"

"What about it? It couldn't kill anyone there could it?"

"No, but it blew all the skeletons up"

We continued with this grisly conversation until we had expounded it to our satisfaction. We knew that most of what we were saying was not true and perhaps that was why we treated it in such as seemingly lighthearted manner. Perhaps we had heard snatches of conversation, perhaps it was our childish imagination at work that made us dream up such horrifying things but, in those days, life was horrifying and, no doubt, in normal times we would never have thought of such dreadful things but now, sadly, we were becoming accustomed to people being killed each night.

With that unique ability of the young, we suddenly put it all out of our minds and decided to play 'tick'. As we played, work was still going on to try and clear the bomb stricken streets and ensure no-one else was still trapped beneath the rubble. Housewives were busy trying to tidy up as best they could. Sweeping brushes were brought out and the debris swept up. Front doorsteps were whitened with donkey stone. Windows might be missing, the brickwork pitted from blast damage, but the cleaning up process continued in a defiant gesture against the enemy.

During the next night, as we settled down in the shelter I cuddled down beneath the blankets and hugged Terry. The raid seemed to go on and on forever. Just as we began to think it was passing over, another wave of bombers descended and it began all over again. I hugged Terry tighter and tighter until he squealed and tried to wriggle free from my grasp. When the all-clear finally sounded we sat for a while, with hot cups of tea, wondering whether or not there would be yet another raid that night. There seemed little point in going back upstairs, we slept the rest of the night away in the shelter.

The next three nights saw more attacks and, on the following night, we suffered one of the worst raids ever with something like three hundred incidents in the area. Many whole nights were spent in the shelter during that dreadful week and one morning I awoke to hear a terrific explosion long after the raid had finally ended.

"Mummy, will we ever see morning?" I asked.

"Don't be soft, it is morning" she replied.

The explosion I heard was from a munition ship in Huskisson Dock which had been loaded with 1,000 tons of high explosive bombs when an inflated barrage balloon had fallen on the forward deck setting the ship alight. Despite the most heroic attempts to put out the fire, whilst enemy planes ceaselessly dive-bombed it, the ship finally blew up at 3.00 a.m. in the morning.

Some very strange sights met our eyes the morning after these raids. One day we awoke to find the whole area covered in white fluffy cottonwool. It was almost as if a minor snowstorm had fallen during the night. I couldn't make out what on earth it was. Mother told me that a lorry must have dropped its load of cottonwool and the wind had scattered it. In fact, it was gun cotton from an ammunition train that had blown up the previous night somewhere in the Clubmoor region. This explosion would have been much worse if it had not been for the heroic action of a number of railwaymen who, literally, took their lives in their hands and uncoupled the rear section of the train and shunted it away before the flames reached it. The wagons they managed to detach contained sea mines.

By now the City was in a dreadful state. Fify one thousand people were homeless, whilst in Bootle, a much smaller area, twenty five thousand lost their homes. Three quarters of the rest centres had been put out of action and special emergency measures had to be taken to billet people in reception towns outside the boundaries of the City.

In the centre of the City a vast amount of damage had been wreaked to the Public Library, the Museum, the Technical College, Lewis's Store and the old Rotunda Theatre, whilst telephone communications were so badly affected that Government Departments in Manchester were cut off and had to rely on wireless communications to mobile wireless stations in Liverpool. The docks were ablaze and several ships were sunk or gutted. Sheds and their contents were destroyed. Liverpool's Head Post Office, the Central and Bank Exchanges, the Mersey Dock Offices, the George Dock Buildings, the Oceanic Buildings, India Buildings and the Corn Exchange were all victims of these terrible May raids.

Many of the people in the hardest hit dockside neighbourhoods began to seek a quiet night's rest by travelling out to Huyton to sleep in the woods and fields and soon lorry after lorry, laden with men, women and children, all with blankets and pillows, were leaving each night for the comparative safety of Huyton. It says much for their spirit for, as they were leaving, they were all laughing and singing.

One of our customers travelled out to stay in Thatto Heath and we were asked if we would like to go. That evening mother packed a small case and, as soon as we had finished our tea, we set off to Thatto Heath and Mr. and Mrs. Roberts.

As we walked up the road, with Terry trotting between us on his lead, we were not alone for dozens of other families were making the trek out of Liverpool for the night. What a motley lot we must have looked as we sought out buses, cars or lorries to take us on our way. Many had dogs trailing behind on leads, others carried a shopping bag out of which came the most dreadful wails and, occasionally, a nose and whisker followed by a paw as an ungrateful cat tried to find a means of escape. Bird cages, covered with cloths, were carried carefully whilst some small boys even clutched hold of, what my mother regarded as very suspicious looking, cardboard boxes with airholes punched in the top.

Buses were few and far between and we were lucky indeed if one happened to come along heading for our destination. Lorry drivers and private cars were extremely helpful and all stopped along the way shouting their destinations.

"Anyone for Thatto Heath?"

"Yes" we shouted and gratefully accepted a lift.

Everyone was only too eager to help each other in those days. Hitler drew us all together in a way he could never have dreamed possible.

When we finally arrived, we were greeted like old friends. Mr. and Mrs. Roberts were an elderly couple and couldn't have made us more welcome had we been their own family. We were very, very grateful for the few nights of peaceful rest we had at their home.

On the morning of 8th May, the all clear sounded and we began to prepare for yet another onslaught that evening, but the enemy had tired before we had and the blitzkrieg was over. Normal life would not be re-established for some time but we got our breath back and were ready to fight on. Some six to seven thousand workmen were sent to help repair the damage, and the Port of Liverpool stayed open — despite Hitler. Now the dreadful toll of casualties and damage began to be assessed.

On 14th May, a mass funeral was held at Anfield Cemetery, when 1,000 victims of the May raids were buried in a common grave. Eighteen firemen were killed, whilst one hundred and eighty were injured fighting the hundreds of fires. Rescue workers got out alive, from under debris, one thousand six hundred and fifty three people who had been buried for anything from three to forty-eight hours. In all, during the month of May, one thousand, four hundred and fifty three people were killed in Liverpool and one thousand and sixty five seriously injured, whilst in the smaller Borough of Bootle, two hundred and fifty seven were killed and twenty six seriously injured.

PHOTOGRAPHIC SECTION TWO

"After the Blitz"

The following 28 pages show some of the devastation created by the War. As you will see, the first 3 pages show 6 panoramas which, on later pages, you will see in more detail.

Captions for the first 3 pages are as follows:

Panorama One and Two:
> *Central Redevelopment Area 1941.*
> *James Street, Brunswick Street – July 1941.*

Panorama Three and Four:
> *Luftwaffe Trail. Centre of Liverpool – May 1941.*
> *Fenwick Street and Corn Exchange, Brunswick Street – August 1941.*

Panorama Five and Six:
> *Hanover Street – August 1941.*
> *Surrey Street, Bootle – October 1941.*

Captions for pages 131-134 are as follows:

View from Castle Street, showing damage caused by enemy action on 3-4 May, 1941, to St. George's Crescent, South Castle Street and Preeson's Row.

57a Drury Lane, looking towards James Street. Shows the White Star Building and in the foreground the ruins of Drury Buildings. Water Street is on the right.

Evacuation of Schoolchildren (2 photographs).

The remaining photographs are captioned individually.

LUFTWAFFE TRAIL

What the centre of Liverpool looked like after the eightnight attack of May, 1941. Compare with air photograph on page 65.

130

131

134

Mossley Hill Church after enemy raid – August 1940.

St. Michael's Church, Pitt Street – 21st September, 1941.

St. Nicholas's Church, Chapel Street. South aisle and Chancel – 21st September, 1941.

St. Luke's Church. Interior, looking west – 9th November 1941.

CHAPTER 12

"Terry Come Home"

12

After the massive onslaught of those first eight nights in May, things began to get a little quieter and we had somewhat of an easier time during the middle and latter part of the month, although enemy raiders were in the vicinity on several occasions. By the end of the month, Merseyside was back in full production again with the Port, the telephone services and the factories working with a greater sense of urgency than ever before.

The clearing up process would go on for many more months, but life was reasonably good and Spring was in the air. On a Sunday people began to make their way to the Park for a quiet stroll in the early sunshine and breathe in some fresh air after all the long nights huddled in stuffy shelters.

One Sunday afternoon we decided to go to Walton Hall Park so, with Terry happily trotting beside us, off we set. Terry, even more than most dogs, was fanatical about playing with anything he could find. A bit of string, an old matchstick, a stone or a ball quickly became a plaything when Terry picked it up. He could spend hours happily tugging on the end of an old bit of string or running after a ball so, naturally, we took a small rubber ball with us and spent some time throwing it for him in the big field. After a while we decided to walk further on and headed up Walton Hall Avenue.

We turned into Stopgate Lane without realising that a large munition factory was sited there and were suddenly surprised to find the road filling up with crowds of people. The factory had just finished one of its shifts and the workers were crowding out on their way home. As they flooded out, some on foot, some on bicycles, the road began to get busier and busier. Big buses stood by waiting to take on the queues of workers and, as they filled up and moved off, they added to the amount of traffic in the road.

"Terry had better go on his lead" decided my father, reaching in his pocket.

Just at that moment, a large dog came up behind us and surprised Terry who shot in front with the dog at his heels. My father called but it was too late, the two dogs ran into the road, there was a squeal of brakes and we saw, to our horror, that a car had hit Terry and flung him on his back amidst the oncoming traffic. I screamed and made to follow but my parents held me back. We watched Terry get up and, in his panic, run further across the road to the other side where a bus struck him down again. The traffic was so heavy now that it obscured our view. When it eventually cleared Terry had disappeared. By now I was almost hysterical and only wanted to dash across the road and find Terry, but my parents held on to me until we were all able to cross in safety.

"He can't be very badly hurt, else he wouldn't have been able to run off like that" mother reasoned. "He's probably very frightened and, in his panic, he's hiding somewhere in the bushes".

We searched and called frantically but could find no sign of him. The crowds began to disperse and we got a better view of the surroundings.

"He may have crossed back again to the other side of the road" my father suggested " Let's go back and look over there".

Back we went to the opposite side of the road but still there was no sign of Terry.

"Do you think he might have run into the factory grounds?" mother asked, as we stood outside calling his name.

"I'll go and see if I can get in and have a look" father said.

He walked up to the man on the gate, but he was refused permission as this was Government property and a high security area where no unauthorised persons were admitted. One of the last few workers leaving the site overheard my father talking to the gateman.

"I'll nip back on my bike and have a look for you" he offered.

We waited anxiously as he cycled back into the grounds. After some time he returned, he'd looked everywhere but there was no sign of Terry.

We were frantic and, after several hours, I had to accept that Terry was lost. Darkness was now beginning to fall and we would have to go home without him. My father promised to come back again the following day and continue the search and, reluctantly, we turned for home.

I cried all the way home whilst my parents tried to comfort me. An advertisement was put in the 'Lost and Found' column of the Liverpool Echo and, for the next three days, we spent all our spare time looking for Terry. During the daytime, Mrs. Malone, one of our neighbours, took me with her and we walked backwards and forwards along Stopgate Lane calling his name. Each evening when my father came home from work, he went off on his bicycle to search.

I cried myself to sleep each night and then, on the Wednesday, we had some good news. One of our customers who worked in the biscuit factory close to where Terry disappeared, reported that she and the other girls had been feeding a little scottie the previous evening. He had wandered into the factory and they had all been delighted with the way he sat up and begged. From her description we were sure it was Terry.

That evening it began to rain so heavily that it was impossible for my father to go out and continue the search. Terry had been missing for three days now and I went to bed sadly wondering if I would ever see him again. Mother came upstairs with me as I got ready and said my prayers — a special one to please bring Terry home safely. My father was downstairs reading the paper. As he sat quietly by himself he heard a peculiar scratching noise at the front door and, setting aside the paper, went to investigate. He opened the door and, to his amazement, a soaking wet bundle of fur flung itself upon him with whimpers of delight — Terry had come home all by himself.

My father could scarcely believe his eyes as he picked the excited dog up and hugged him.

"Terry's come home" he yelled at the top of his voice.

I was out of bed in a flash and rushing down the stairs followed closely by my mother.

With tears of joy pouring down my face, I hugged Terry to me regardless of his soaking wet fur. He, in turn, struggled and wriggled and licked my face. Once I had set him free he ran round shaking himself and rubbing his coat on the rug. Mother fetched some old towels and tried to rub him dry but he was so excited he couldn't stand still long enough to allow her to dry him.

It was sometime before we all settled down again that evening but, eventually, I went back to bed. Terry curled up happily at the foot, whilst I, still hardly able to believe he was safe, snuggled down and for the first time in three nights, slept on a dry pillow. How he had ever managed to find his own way home would always be a mystery, but he had and that was all that mattered.

Thankfully, we were free of air-raids during the time Terry was lost but, a week after his return, the sirens went again and we were back to the old routine, fearful in case another blitzkrieg was on its way. Although some of the raids were heavy, they were nothing like that dreadful first week in May and, finally, the month gave way to June with a raid that brought forth a spate of Ack-Ack and aerial machine gun fire, during which flares and incendiary bombs were dropped, but no serious damage was done.

During the month of June, we had about seven raids in which incendiary bombs were dropped and some damage was caused by high explosives. However, the worst seemed to be over and gradually, the workmen moved in to repair some of the damage.

Bank Holidays were no longer recognised now for, such was the need for high productivity in all the factories, most worked to a shift pattern all through the usual holiday period. Even the annual summer holiday had changed as people were encouraged to take their holidays at home.

Travel was extremely difficult as the railways were needed for the transport of essential goods and supplies and even the armed forces found it difficult to get a decent seat on a train when returning to their units after a short leave.

We were lucky on Merseyside, for there were many beauty spots in the surrounding area where you could happily spend a day picnicking and playing. During my father's annual holiday he and my mother took it in turns to have days out. We enjoyed many happy days at Raby Mere, Thurstaston, Parkgate and New Brighton.

On one such day mother and I decided to go to Raby Mere and I invited a friend along for company. As we sailed across the familiar Mersey the sea was calm and smooth and we filled our lungs with the salty fresh air. Around us the river was, as usual, full of shipping but now they no longer sported the gay colours of pre-war days for they were all painted in a dark grey camouflage against enemy aircraft and submarines. Above them flew huge barrage balloons to stop dive bombers. In the distance we could make out the mast and rails of the 'Royal Daffodil' sunk by enemy action and now tied up alongside Seacombe Ferry. Up and down the river were 'wreck' warnings denoting the sites of other sunken vessels.

"Are there any mines in the Mersey?" I asked.

"Shouldn't think so" mother replied with a smile.

"Well, how did all those ships get sunk then?"

"They'll be the ones that got bombed during the blitz" mother replied as our boat bumped up against the sleepers at Woodside Ferry.

There was no time to ask any more questions. We trooped downstairs to the lower deck just in time to see the large gangplank thump down on to the lower deck and then we were off amidst the crowds wending their way up the steep slope to the turnstiles at the top.

We walked across the fields from Bromborough to Raby Mere where we picnicked by the mere and threw the remains of our sandwiches to the ever hungry ducks who waddled up to scrounge what they could. Later, we began to make our way home. Walking alongside a stream I suddenly found myself sinking in the mud. I grabbed my friend and very soon we were both up to our knees and shouting to my mother for help. Mother soon pulled us on to firmer ground only to discover that I had lost a shoe in the mud. Armed with some sticks we poked around in the foul smelling mud until finally the missing shoe was retrieved.

By now we were in a dreadful mess. Our legs and feet were covered in the thick brown slime, our socks ruined, our shoes a mess. We cleaned ourselves up as best we could, but it was very uncomforable walking back to the bus in our wet shoes. However, we were even more embarrassed when we got on the bus for the mud smelt foul and, whilst not too noticeable in the fresh air, it was overpowering within the confines of the bus. We found ourselves on the receiving end of many strange looks and were very glad indeed when we eventually arrived home.

In normal times we would have looked forward to a long soak in a luxurious hot bath but now we were only allowed $5\frac{1}{2}''$ of water in a bath so we just had to clean off the worst with a bowl of warm water before getting into the shallow bath.

Our shoes were ruined, which did not please our mothers, for it meant precious clothing coupons would have to be spent on a new pair. As from 1st June, clothes rationing had come into operation and that meant coupons for all clothes, cloth and footwear. Each person was allowed 66 coupons per year and as a pair of shoes cost five coupons, it was not surprising our mothers were none too happy.

By now the shortages were really hitting home. Our food was rationed, our clothing rationed and the men found, to their horror, that not only were cigarettes in very short supply but the pubs were running short of beer!

The whole advertising scene underwent a change as the large grocers such as Irwins and the Co-operative Society began advertising to encourage customers to re-register with them for service and civility rather than for the goods they had to sell. The Government itself became one of the largest advertisers of all as they advertised for 'Recruits for Factories', 'Building Workers', 'War Savings', and 'Food Facts' in addition to their Public Information adverts.

Suddenly however, a new spate of advertising hit us as 'Victory V' signs began sprouting up all over Liverpool. There wasn't a street, railway station or large building without a large batch of prominently displayed 'V's. They were chalked and painted everywhere, even on the underside of high railway bridges. This phenomena was not confined to Liverpool, but was rife throughout the whole country.

Searchlight batteries were even making the 'V' sign in the skies as they searched for enemy planes during the hours of darkness. Clerks and secretaries found them suddenly appearing on letters. In reality it was a symbol of loyalty. The makers of Victory V lozenges must have been exultant.

At the end of August even milk was rationed and, as the summer waned, thoughts began to turn to the dark nights ahead and all this could bring. The air-raid season was coming and there was still a great possibility of invasion.

Our own bombers had not been inactive during the last few weeks, for heavy raids on Kiel, Hanover, Brunswick and Magdelburg were reported and, for the first time, our bombers had actually penetrated and bombed Berlin itself. The Luftwaffe, meantime, had been unable to sustain the heavy air-raids over England due to the Russian offensive.

German Forces had attacked the frontier on the whole front from the Baltic to the Black Sea, bringing Russia into the war against Germany and it was probably this fact that had saved us from invasion. That the war was escalating there was no doubt, as reports came through of large numbers of our troops being evacuated from Crete and landed in the Middle East.

It seemed now there was no stopping Hitler in his attempt to take over the world.

CHAPTER 13

"Stocking The Larder"

13

America, whilst sending goods and supplies to this country under the Lease and Lend Act, had still not entered the war. Churchill and Roosevelt (the American President), had met and talked secretly and there was a great deal of speculation as to whether or not they would now take their place alongside us in the fight against Nazism.

The air-raids seemed to be slackening off for, during the whole of August and September, we had only two visits from the Luftwaffe. The great fear now was that whilst the extra daylight of summer had afforded us some protection, the long winter evenings ahead would bring the bombers back again in full force.

Everyone was still talking about the terrible May blitz and, as we prepared for winter, more and more news came through of the heroism displayed by so many Merseysiders.

The Hospital service had even more reason to be proud of its record of service when the story of the bombing of Mill Road Hospital became known. During the height of a raid it had the misfortune to be one of the early victims and four hundred patients had to be transferred to other hospitals. The X-Ray Unit, the Emergency Unit and the Ambulance Station had all been demolished whilst, in the Operating Theatre, an emergency operation had actually been in progress. The surgeon was killed and the sister buried in the debris, her body not being recovered until some days later. The patient, covered in debris, was rescued by porters, sisters, nurses and A.R.P. workers and driven three miles through the blitzed areas to another hospital where the operation was completed.

Many of Liverpool's fine buildings had been badly damaged by fire. All that remained of the historic old parish church St. Nicholas' at the Pier Head was the tower, spire, vestry and some blackened walls, whilst that other fine old church, St. Luke's, at the top of Bold Street, was completely gutted by fire.

As the first chill winds of Autumn sent us searching out last year's woollens, my mother tried to store as much food as possible against the winter months, for she knew that it would be then that the food shortage would hit the hardest.

All during the summer I had helped with the bottling of fruit and jamming. Not much fruit was made into jam because of the shortage of sugar, but when the strawberries apeared, red and luscious, my mother agreed to make a couple of pounds.

"Is that another strawberry you've just had?" mother asked suspiciously as I helped hull and wash them.

I could hardly deny I had taken one when my cheek was still bulging.

"If you don't leave them alone, there'll be none left for the jam" I was warned.

I couldn't help thinking how marvellous it must have been, before the war, to go into the grocers and just ask for a couple of pounds of sugar without having to worry about ration books. We could have made all the strawberry jam we wanted then.

"Don't be silly, of course you couldn't. You still had to pay for the sugar" mother told me.

I hadn't thought of that. All that seemed to matter nowadays were the ration books, the points and the coupons.

"You can't have any more socks, there's no more coupons left"

"No, we can't have tinned fruit for tea, I've no more points"

"Go easy with the butter, that's the last of the ration"

At one time it would have been "I've no more money left" or "It's too dear", now points and coupons were even more precious and hard to come by than the money in our pockets.

The storing of food was not so simple during the war years for few ordinary folk had refrigerators, and freezers were a luxury no ordinary home could enjoy. Bottling and drying was a very necessary chore if you wanted to store the fruits of summer away for the winter.

Mother used to dry apples and store them in air-tight containers. She peeled and cored the apples, sliced them into rings and then heated them in a solution of salt water. After this, they were carefully placed on trays and put into a warm oven to dry out.

"Run in and spread those apple rings out for me before they go cold" she would ask when called into the shop in the middle of the task.

I hated the feel of the apple rings, they were like chamois leather and made me cringe. I was not familiar with the word 'cringe', however, and could only complain that they 'made waves go all over me'.

Sometimes when the meat ration had been used, we had to make do with hot soup and dumplings as a main meal. Even eggs were rationed now and were sorely missed, for there's nothing more versatile than an egg. Egg and Chips, puddings, custards, as well as the familiar old boiled egg for breakfast, were all out of the question. Mother used to buy a packet of 'Creamola' and make a pudding with it. It was yellow in colour, creamy in texture and I loved it.

Mothers strove desperately hard to feed their families as best they could and were as anxious as the Government to maintain the nation's health. One morning a postcard arrived with the usual morning post.

"This is really for you" mother said "It's an appointment to go to the Clinic for your innoculation"

"When do I have to go?" I asked.

"Friday afternoon" Mother told me.

"Will it hurt?"

"No, it's just a quick jab and its all over. Much better than risk getting Diptheria".

I had to agree with this. Young as I was, I knew the dreadful scourge Diptheria was amongst children at that time. Almost 3,000 children died from it each year. As the winter months were the most dangerous for this particular disease, the Ministry of Health had set about a massive campaign to have all children between the ages of 1 and 15 innoculated, free of charge, with a new vaccine that had just become available.

Friday morning and I was queuing up alongside dozens of other children, our sleeves rolled up, waiting for the miraculous jab that would save us from the dreaded disease. Thankfully, due to innoculation, it is rare indeed to hear of a case today.

It was to the everlasting credit of the people of Liverpool, and not least the women, that there were no outbreaks of disease at that time for, with all the debris and rubble left from the bombing, these areas could quickly have become breeding grounds for all sorts of unpleasant germs. We were continually being warned to keep away from the bomb sites and often the familiar phrase;

"Don't go near there, it's alive with dead rats" would ring out.

The women cleaned and polished, swept and scrubbed and the local chandlers shop did a good trade in 'soft soap' and 'aunt sally'. I had always loved scrubbing floors and, as a very small child, used to worry Mrs. Close, our neighbour, to let me go and scrub her front step. Living in a shop, we did not have the usual front door and it was a great treat when, armed with bucket and brush, I was allowed to go next door and scrub the steps. Part of the pleasure of this was using 'soft soap'. It was brown, thick and slimy and was bought loose from the chandlers, customers taking along their own jam jar into which the soap was poured. It was delightful to use, or at least I thought so. It smelt strongly of carbolic and I loved plunging my hand into the gooey mess and extracting a handful which, after plopping it on to the wet floor, soon worked up into a fine lather.

The chandlers shop was a veritable joy in itself with all the mingling aromas of soap, disinfectants, firelighters and paraffin. The latter was sold loose, as were most things those days, and people would bring large cans into which the required amount was poured. 'Aunt Sally', a strong, red liquid soap (also used for washing floors), was carefully measured out by the pint or half pint and then poured into a jam jar. With so few goods pre-packaged it was possible, in those days, to close your eyes and still be able to tell, just by the smell, which shop you were in.

Detergents had yet to be introduced, as had washing-up liquid. The only washing machine available to most folk was the old dolly tub and boiler. Much of the washing had to be done by hand.

Every washday, mother would sort the clothes into separate piles. The whites would be put into the boiler to which she added pieces of 'Acdo', carefully cut from the main block, or alternatively, pieces of hard soap. Most of the other clothes would be washed by hand. This was a laborious job for each article had to be rubbed and squeezed in the hot soapy water and then rinsed several times to make sure all the soap had gone.

Once the whites had boiled, they were then transferred to the sink for rinsing, then they had to be starched and blued. The kettle was put on to boil, whilst mother put a few handfuls of starch into a large bowl and mixed it to a thick cream with some cold water. After this, the boiling water was added until the starch 'turned'. 'Turning' was when the water turned clear.

Different strengths of starch were used for the various articles being washed. Collars required a very strong mixture so always went in first. Tablecloths, pillowcases and teatowels came next, followed by shirts, blouses and last of all, handkerchiefs. Before the starching commenced, a 'blue bag' was squeezed into the mixture several times turning the water a dark blue in colour. This was to ensure the 'whites' came out a really dazzling white.

Finally, it was through the mangle with the lot as each garment was fed carefully into the big rollers and the handle turned to squeeze out as much moisture as possible. Some hours later, after the clothes had blown merrily in the breeze on the long clothes line outside, they would be brought in and carefully folded, in readiness for ironing. Some of the starched items stuck together and you had to run your hand through to separate them. Every single item was carefully ironed, folded and hung up to air on large racks strung high on the ceiling. There was no such thing as 'drip-dry' in those days.

As soon as the washing was finished, the sink would need attention and this would be scoured with 'monkey stone' until it was shining like a new pin. There was no plastic, everything was made of wood and this required much scrubbing to keep it in the clean, white pristine condition beloved by every housewife.

What with the housework, the queuing for food and the essential work outside the home still to be undertaken, no wonder our mothers found themselves working harder than ever before and, often, with very little sleep.

Some form of recreation was essential and the pictures were never more popular. Long queues formed outside as each evening people waited to get in. Before the big picture started there was nearly always a 'Ministry of Information' film which consisted mainly of warnings to the public about the possibility of spies in the area and how to recognise them, the dangers of careless talk and the possibility of gas attacks and how to cope.

To everyone's relief there had not, as yet, been any gas attacks but the authorities were ever mindful of the possibility and gas exercises were organised, at regular intervals, in all the big cities.

One day, mother and I had gone to Southport and were happily walking along Lord Street when, suddenly, I saw a large placard warning people that a 'mock gas attack' would take place at six o'clock that evening. Panic stricken, I begged mother to let us get the next train home. All the reassurance in the world couldn't convince me that they would not use real gas and we hadn't got our gas masks with us. Suffice to say that my fear was so great we actually did catch the next train home.

CHAPTER 14

"Dig For Victory"

14

As the year 1941 drew to a close, it seemed the war was still not going well for us. The air attacks on Merseyside were now almost over. The sirens had gone several times during October and November but little aamage was done, mainly due to the fact that we had new defences and these quickly went into action backed up by the night fighters. The last raid of the year took place in November, when after an interval of a week, we had a night attack. It was later disclosed that the bombers were now carrying a fender or girder on their noses as a defence against our Balloon Barrage but as these weighed between 600 to 800 pounds, they slowed up the machine and reduced the bomb and petrol load they could carry and made it almost impossible to fly on one engine so that a twin engined machine, crippled in one motor, would have to come down. The Luftwaffe was losing the battle.

Whilst the Germans might be losing the battle in the skies, the battle of the Atlantic still waged on and the U-Boats did a great deal of damage to the ships bringing in our essential supplies. Vast convoys sailed in and out of Liverpool and the Port became one of the major troop transit areas.

My mother was always fearful for the safety of my cousin who was in the Royal Navy and for whom I was still busy trying to knit that wretched scarf that seemed never to grow.

One day, whilst serving in the shop, we saw a Naval Padre come in and stand at the back. When it came to his turn to be served he declined saying he would wait. Mother couldn't clear the shop quickly enough.

"Slip the lock on for a minute love" she said to me as she tok the Padre through to the living room.

I waited in the shop and presently they came out.

"Put the kettle on for me, I'm just going next door for a minute" mother said.

I could see she was upset as, together, she and the Padre went out. It was some time before mother returned and I asked what had happened. Mother told me that our next door neighbour's son had been reported missing, presumed killed. He, also, was in the Royal Navy and his ship had been torpedoed. No doubt the family would go on hoping for many weeks that he might have survived and be a Prisoner of War. Sadly, that was not the case.

Seafaring was an old tradition in Liverpool, so it was not surprising that many of the men were in either the Royal Navy or the Merchant Service. In addition, many ships were built on the Mersey including the most famous of all, the Ark Royal, which had by now fallen victim to a U-Boat. When Warship Week took place from 15th to 22nd November, the people gave generously. "Liverpool" said the Lord Mayor when opening the Appeal "had suffered very heavily and very gallantly as a result of the enemy air attacks and it never pays to hit a Liverpudlian".

Christmas was coming once again and it seemed as though it would be another bleak, cheerless festival, for nobody felt there was much to celebrate.

We got out our decorations and I began to sort out those we could still use. With the paper shortage having now reached an acute stage, there was not even any hope of purchasing crepe paper or strips of the brightly coloured gummed paper with which we once used to fashion our own garlands.

Our school books had now taken on a new appearance as the pure white pages gave way to brown and grey with black speckles all over them. All waste paper had to be re-cycled and used over and over again and the black speckles were merely the remains of the old print. I spent hours trying to find letters and words amongst the speckles.

We began to find other ways of making decorations. Old cardboard milk bottle tops were painted and hung on the tree or covered with bits of wool to make pom-poms. Anyone with a garden was lucky, for they might have laurel leaves and other evergreens. We scoured the parks for acorns and pine cones and these we dabbed with whitewash to resemble snow.

Gifts were another problem, even a box of handkerchiefs cost precious coupons.

"What can I buy for mummy?" I asked my father.

"Oh, we'll think of something don't worry" he said. He didn't know either I thought.

Amidst our preparations, we suddenly received the stunning news that Japan had attacked Pearl Harbour. To me, the Japanese were a completely different kettle of fish from the Germans. I was quite, quite sure in my mind that if ever a Japanese soldier popped his head round City Road and came face to face with me I would just die of sheer terror.

"I don't know what you're worrying about, they're thousands of miles away from us" my parents told me.

I just hoped they stayed thousands of miles away from us.

With the attack on Pearl Harbour, America now entered the war and I remember feeling somewhat glad that it would be them not us that would be fighting the Japanese. Little did I realise that many, many of our own men would be fighting the bitter war in the jungles of the Far East. When it did finally dawn on me I felt very, very sorry for them. In my eyes they really had the worst job of all.

Christmas passed quietly that year as families grieved for those they had lost and others worried about their near and dear ones far away from home. As the New Year dawned, we fervently hoped and prayed it would bring better news.

After Christmas I, like many other children, had 'Gift Tokens' to spend. These were something new and were the brain child of the large stores who had put their heads together and, anxious not to lose the Christmas trade, come up with this new and novel idea. No coupons were needed by the purchaser of the Voucher, whilst the recipients could obtain coupon controlled goods, if desired, by giving up their own coupons at the time the Vouchers were being exchanged.

As we travelled into town to spend our Tokens I found a new game to play. Instead of countng the 'Mary Ellens', I tried to guess the nationality of the servicemen who thronged the busy streets. Liverpool had always been known as a cosmopolitan City but it was never more so than now. The French were easy to spot for they always wore a red pom pom on their berets. The Australian and New Zealanders wore large hats with one side folded up against the crown. The others were not so easy to distinguish and I puzzled long and hard to decide which were Czech, Polish, Dutch or Russian.

"If I catch you leaving the soap in the water any more there's going to be trouble" mother warned me one morning after I had finished washing.

"It was only a little piece" I protested.

"It doesn't matter how small it was, we can't afford to waste it. Put it in the jar on the draining board in future"

In February, no doubt to the delight of all small boys, soap rationing came into operation. Soap could only be bought against a coupon or buying permit. No more leaving the soap in the water to get soft. Now we had to save every scrap.

We were not the only ones to have a jar on the draining board for all the bits. They were carefully hoarded in readiness for making a new piece.

As soon as we had sufficient bits, mother put them into a pan, with a little water and placed it on the stove to heat. The resultant jelly like mixture was then poured into a small basin or other suitable receptacle. The final result of this procedure was a mound of soap, softer than usual, which could be used for washing and help save precious coupons for another new bar. We were developing into a very ingenious nation when it came to ways of making the rations go further.

One night, fast asleep in bed, I was awoken by mother gently shaking me. I opened my eyes "The sirens haven't gone off have they?" I asked incredulously for we had not had a raid for sometime now.

"No, the siren's haven't gone" she said. I could hear voices downstairs.

"Come on, slip your dressing gown on" she said.

I got up, wriggled into my dressing gown and shoved my feet into my slippers.

Downstairs I discovered my cousin and his fiancee had arrived. He was on leave from the Royal Navy and the exciting news was they were planning to get married.

I was delighted. We were going to a wedding.

Of course the adults had all the headaches when it came to planning a wartime wedding, we children just enjoyed the fun. Rations had to be carefully saved and hoarded for the reception. Clothing coupons carefully counted so that a new outfit could be purchased.

When the big day finally dawned and we arrived back at my Aunties for the reception, the Wedding Cake took pride of place on the table. It looked exactly like a traditional Wedding cake but it hid one big secret — there was no icing sugar on it!

Icing sugar was unobtainable so the bakers had come up with an especially good brainwave. They simply made a white cardboard cover to slip over the cake and this they decorated with all the usual trimmings. This clever deception only came to light when it was time for the Bride and Groom to 'cut the cake', then the cover had to be removed in order for them to cut the first slice. Only those lucky enough to have relatives abroad, kind enough to send a cake on to them, managed the real thing. So unusual was it to see these lovely three tiered iced cakes that they almost took pride of place in the photographs and were even featured in the local papers.

CHAPTER 15

"America Enters The War"

15

During 1942 the Invasion came, but it wasn't the Germans. They never managed to set foot on the mainland, although they did occupy the Channel Islands. This invasion was by our allies — the Americans, who came over at the rate of about 20,000 a week.

Before arriving in this country, the American troops were warned that, although we might look dowdy and badly dressed by their standards, it was due to the rationing and not our lack of interest in good clothes and fashion. Alike in so many ways, suddenly we were to find out what differences there were between us.

Although both countries spoke basic English, some of the expressions used by the G.I's, as we called them, were very strange to us. No doubt we sounded just as peculiar to them. Naturally, it was the children who picked up the American 'slang' the quickest.

Some people welcomed the Americans, some merely put up with them whilst others took an intense dislike to them and whatever they did. They were certainly different, these strangers from across the Atlantic. To the conservative English, they seemed to be brash, over talkative and 'show-offs'. They had more money, smarter uniforms, access to all sorts of luxuries we had not seen for some time and, they were very popular with the girls. It was probably the latter that made them so unpopular with our own men.

It had long been known that anyone with relatives in America were lucky indeed. Often they would be on the receiving end of a parcel containing such luxuries as silk stockings, cigarettes, chewing gum, tinned fruit, tinned meat and other goodies.

One of the girls in our class was the lucky recipient of some of these goodies when her brother, who was serving in the Navy, came home on leave after a visit to America. When she opened a box containing chewing gum, lifesaver sweets, pen nibs — very, very scarce in this country — and some bars of American chocolate, she instantly became the most popular girl in the class.

"Can I have some?" one cheeky lad asked blatantly.

"There's only enough for my friends" she said firmly.

"I'll be your friend" he offered.

"You never play with us, you're always with that crowd over there".

"Well, I'll play with you lot today if you give us some chewy"

Finally relenting, the girl broke a small piece off a long strip of chewing gum and gave it to him.

"Hey, look what I've got . . . chewy" he crowed running back to his own pals.

"Where'd you get that?" they demanded.

"She's got loads over there. Her brother's just come home from America and you should see what he's brought"

They came to see.

As soon as she had managed to extricate herself from the crowd, the remains of the chewing gum was carefully shared out, as were the lifesavers. I was the lucky recipient of one of the pen nibs. What luxury, it was too good to use every day so, after a quick try out, away it went to be carefully saved for the end of term examinations, when our very best handwriting would be called for.

Apart from these personal packages, America sent many consumable goods in addition to ammunitions and 'Liberty' boats. Amongst these goods were tinned foods such as fruit, dried eggs, bacon and spam. My father loved bacon for breakfast but, with the rationing, had to be content with bacon on Sunday and toast the rest of the week. When the tinned bacon appeared on sale mother was delighted. I was despatched off, ration book in hand, to buy two tins.

"Have you tried it yet?" the girl in the shop asked me.

"No"

'It's awfully fatty" she warned.

She certainly wasn't wrong. When the tin was opened it consisted of nearly all fat wrapped around strips of greaseproof paper. It 'plopped' out of the tin in one greasy lump and, whilst the fat was useful for frying bread in, the amount of meat was negligible.

"Oh well, never mind" mother said philosophically "and there was me thinking what a treat it would be".

The 'spam' was better, quite tasty I thought. Not only could you buy it in tins, but the shop also cut it into slices and I often ran over to the Co-op and bought two ounces for our lunch. Mother was not so keen, it was a bit spicy for her. Dried egg was another favourite with me, especially made into an omelette.

"I don't know, you've got some peculiar tastes" mother told me.

The raids over Merseyside had now ceased, the last bomb falling on the City on the 10th January, 1942. The Civil Defence did not allow their efficiency or keenesss to fall for they were ever mindful that there was always the danger that the enemy would return or try a different strategy so, air-raid drill and fire watching rotas were still faithfully adhered to and a campaign to recruit women into the fire watching scheme was begun.

As the lighter nights of Spring arrived, we were able to spend more time playing out. With the absence of traffic, due to the petrol rationing, roller skating became one of our favourite pastimes. We were able to skate to our hearts content without the worry of traffic.

At the top of City Road was a bridge over the railway line which was known locally as the 'brew'. This was a favourite spot for skating and many, many happy hours were spent making our way laboriously to the top just for the pleasure of rolling down again.

I commenced skating with a pair of 'blocks' but soon wanted the more sophisticated version that many of my friends already possessed — ball bearings. With a pair of 'ball-bearings' you could skate faster and smoother and many of the youngsters were skilled indeed at turning and stopping and executing all manner of intricate steps and twirls. I began to worry my parents for a pair.

"All the others have got them" I argued, using the well known strategy that all children have employed throughout the ages.

Eventually, I too was the proud possessor of a pair of 'ball-bearing' skates. Now I too could learn to skate as fast as the others and do all the fascinating tricks they enjoyed. Of course this was strictly 'fair weather' activity and we were often 'rained off'. However, like all youngsters, we quickly found other things with which to occupy our time. If we couldn't find anything to do our mothers found it for us.

"The Devil makes work for idle hands" mother said.

The work on making good the bomb damage was still progressing but, with so much to be done, the replacement of windows came very low down on the list of priorities. Consequently, our shop window had still not been replaced and the area was useless for displaying goods as only a small square of glass, measuring about 3 ft x 3 ft, existed in the middle of the dark grey asbestos boarding that secured the shop front.

I soon discovered that the window made a marvellous place for me to play 'house' and quickly took it over for that purpose. The actual window was screened from the shop by a sliding door and the only means of entry was by a ladder. This didn't bother me in the slightest, I just pretended it was the 'front door'. I scrounged a small rug off my mother, borrowed a little table and these, together with a small chair, comprised my furniture. Many happy hours were spent dusting and polishing my little house.

One day I managed to persuade mother to let me have a small plant to put on the table but this proved to be a grave mistake on my part for the conditions in the window were ideal for plants. When mother saw how well my plant was growing she realised just what potential the window held for growing other things. With the 'Dig for Victory' campaign so intense, mother decided to grow her own tomatoes — in the window.

Soon my little house was converted into a greenhouse as a dozen tomato plants were purchased, potted up and given pride of place. The tomatoes thrived under mother's care as she watered them, fed them and even dusted them with a little rabbit's foot to ensure good pollination.

When, at last, the tiny green fruit began to form we looked forward to our own tomatoes. They did not all ripen as well as they should, but this did not deter mother for she simply picked them, wrapped them in brown paper and tucked them away in a drawer. Some time later she brought them out, the skins had by now turned to a very respectable rosy red.

Much encouraged by these efforts, mother began to wonder what else could be grown at home.

"If we don't watch out she'll be growing cabbages in window boxes and onions in buckets" my father joked.

"What about potatoes in socks?" I ventured.

"Alright, alright. Very funny" father said.

There was much to be said for homegrown produce as greenstuffs had risen rapidly in price. Much of this was due to the fact that there was a general shortage throughout the country. Pre-war consumption had been maintained by importing goods from abroad but now no-one wanted to risk the lives of sailors to bring in goods that could be grown at home.

It was getting more and more difficult to plan a balanced diet and mothers were often at their wits ends to know what to give the family.

"I don't know what on earth we're going to have for our tea tonight" they complained.

"Did you see that menu in the paper the other day?"

"Which one was that?"

"You know, in 'Food Facts' "

"No, what was it?"

"Suggesting porridge, potato cakes and milk for breakfast. Vegetable soup, cheese and potato pie or something for lunch and raw grated carrot sandwiches for tea. I ask you. It's supposed to be the ideal meal for a two to six year old. You tell me how you persuade them to eat it?"

"Got no idea have they?"

"You can say that again"

There were long queues at all the food shops now. Mother couldn't leave the shop to queue but we had very good neighbours who queued on her behalf. With meat being so scarce, and strictly rationed, it was impossible to share our small meals with our pets. Horsemeat became the answer to that problem.

The pet shop on County Road got regular supplies of horsemeat for the local cat and dog population and, of course, there was always the inevitable queue outside, long before the delivery van was even due. Mrs. Ellis, one of our customers queued regularly for meat for both our dog and her own. The meat was very like ordinary stewing steak but, of course, was not supposed to be fit for human consumption.

We had a good laugh one day when Mrs. Ellis came back and related a conversation she had overheard in the queue. Apparently, two woman had been discussing the difficulties of providing a good hot dinner each day and one, in particular, had a problem in that her husband, a big burly docker, demanded meat every day and ranted and raved at her if he did not get it.

"Well" she told the queue "I've had enough of that. If he wants meat every day he can have meat every day — horsemeat. He can't tell the difference. Last night he mopped the gravy up with a piece of dry bread and said it was lovely. That'll teach him."

However, it was often suspected that horsemeat found its way on to other tables and eventually the government passed a law whereby it should all be dyed green so that it could not be passed off as ordinary meat to an unsuspecting public.

For those with money it was still possible to eat out, as restaurants and hotels continued to provide food. A lot of ill feeling grew about those people able to live in hotels on a permanent basis and it was often suspected that they received more food than the rest of us.

Anyone living in a Hotel could have anything they liked from the menu, regardless of the 5/-d limit imposed on meals in restaurants. Such was the disquiet over the situation that it was eventually announced that an 'Official Eye' would be kept on the situation in future.

It was almost as though we were obsessed with the food shortages and every week new announcements were made concerning our present or future food supplies.

CHAPTER 16

"The Lodge"

16

We were now able to get a decent night's sleep, without the fear of being dragged from our warm beds into the shelter each night. This was not the case in Europe, however, for the R.A.F. were now involved in a heavy bombing programme on Germany and other strategic targets in occupied Europe.

In one month, British aircraft made over 7,700 flights during daylight sweeps over occupied France and an average of 250 fighter aircraft were engaged in the air offensive every day.

How dreadful it must have been for the ordinary citizens. Not only was their homeland occupied by the enemy, bringing with it all the horrors that such an occupation entailed, but they were also being subjected to air-raids from us, their Allies, in order to destroy the military objectives set up in their country by the invading forces.

Although we did not have to contend with the air-raids, the war was biting very hard where our supplies were concerned. Most of our food was rationed, as were clothes and soap, and now even more consumable items began to find their way into the rationing scheme. Condensed milk and breakfast cereals went on points and sweet rationing was to commence in July 1942.

My mother had to go down to the Food Office and register. She and the other shopkeepers received vouchers to enable them to purchase initial stocks and, subsequently, the loose sweet coupons would have to be deposited back at the Food Office where more vouchers would be issued in accordance with the number of coupons submitted.

"Come on now, get off the table. I've got the coupons to count"

Oh no! With sinking heart I would clear away my games and then mother would tip out a large box of loose coupons.

"You can give me a hand with these as well. Count them into bundles of fifties first".

It was a fiddly job and always took a couple of hours, even with the three of us counting. Soon, however, the table was covered with neat little stacks of coupons all tied up with string. These were then counted into one big envelope and the details entered on the special forms provided by the Food Office.

Next day, Mother and I set off for the Food Office and waited in the long queue outside. We queued for everything these days. Once inside, we found that counters had been set up with large notices over the top on which were printed letters. Naturally there was a queue at each one and we tagged on to the end of the one showing the initial letter of our surname.

"I wish they'd hurry up, the 'Echoes' will be in" Mother said to me.

"You'd think they had to print the Vouchers as well, the time they take" moaned the man in front of us.

"I'm just worried in case we're late for the papers" mother said.

"Here, they're opening another counter, come on" the man called.

Luckily for us, another assistant had arrived and now two were counting.

Mother was always anxious lest we should be late getting back and the evening papers would arrive before us.

Many times this happened but our paper boys were very good and, as we approached the shop, we would see them sitting on the big bundles of 'Echos' . Those who knew their 'rounds' off by heart, and did not have to have each paper marked for them with the correct address, would have already started counting out the number of papers they required and were often ready to go out on their 'rounds'.

It was always a rush at tea-time with the papers to get out and the shop full of customers waiting to be served. I liked to help serve but I hated it when one of the paper boys didn't turn in and I would have to help with the delivery.

On one such occasion, mother had promised to take me to the pictures to see Laurel and Hardy in 'Air-Raid Wardens'. My father would be late home from work so mother and I planned an early tea as soon as the shop was closed and then, straight to the pictures.

I helped to serve whilst mother marked up the papers as quickly as she could and then we realised that one of the boys hadn't turned in. As the last one left with his 'round', mother glanced at the clock.

"It doesn't look as if Tony's coming in. We'll give him another ten minutes and if he hasn't arrived by then, we'll have to take them ourselves" she said.

"But what about the pictures?" I cried.

"We'll see how long it takes to deliver these and, if there's still time, we might be able to make it. We can have something to eat afterwards."

It was a dreadful night, the rain was pelting down and gusts of wind added to our problems as we set off, armed with a torch, to help find our way in the blackout.

Only anyone who has experience of delivering newspapers can appreciate just how difficult a job it can be. Some houses are not numbered, which means counting each house to ensure the right paper goes into the right letterbox. Letterboxes themselves can be a nightmare. Some are high, some low, some have springs so strong they either trap your fingers or rip the papers. Other doors have no letterboxes and you have to push the paper under the door, often right into the jaws of Fido, the family dog, who waits on the other side, ready to rip the whole thing up.

Occasionally, a gust of wind can catch one of the papers and send it flying up the road into the nearest puddle. It was usually one of mine that went off on a flight up the road, much to mother's despair.

"For goodness sake be careful" she pleaded "we'll have dozens of complaints in the morning if people don't get their papers".

In due time, most of the papers were delivered and we had only the "Lodge" to do. For me, the "Lodge" held all sorts of hidden terrors, for it was situated just inside Anfield Cemetery. Mother and I stood on the pavement waiting to cross Walton Lane, straining our eyes in the blackout to see when the road was clear. As soon as we thought it safe we made our way over by torchlight. Suddenly, I realised mother had disappeared from my side.

"Mummy!" I cried looking round in the darkness, for the torch had now gone and I could hardly see a thing.

Mother's voice came from below.

"I've tripped over the kerb"

I peered down into the inky darkness and could just see my mother lying on the floor. Walton Lane was quite a wide road with tramtracks down the centre. There was a small parapet either side of the tramtrack and it was here mother had tripped.

I helped to get her up and we managed to retrieve the torch and then, with a little help from me, mother hobbled to the pavement. Her knee was badly cut and bleeding, her stockings torn into a large hole and her skirt and coat wet from the rain.

"You take these whilst I see if I can clean this up a bit" she said, handing me the papers for the "Lodge".

I took them reluctantly for I was far from keen on going to the "Lodge" on my own. However, the thought of going to the pictures was still uppermost in my mind and I knew I had better not argue.

I went up to the big heavy iron gates of the cemetery and pushed. It was fearfully dark inside and the gates squeaked ominously as they rolled back. I took a few tentative steps inside and glanced over to the left where the "Lodge" stood, dark and hideous like something out of a horror film. If I ran all the way and threw the papers into the porch I could make it there and back in a few minutes before anything horrible had time to catch me, I thought.

"Alright there?" a deep voice murmured in my ear and I nearly died of sheer terror as I turned around to find an old man in a raincoat standing by my side.

"Here, I didn't frighten you did I?" he looked at me with concern.

Frighten me. He'd nearly scared me to death. In the excitement of mother falling over and the realisation that I would have to go to the "Lodge" on my own, I had forgotten all about the old watchman who had his hut in the bushes just inside the big gates and, in the darkness, I hadn't noticed him when I came in.

My mouth was dry and my heart pounding as he spoke to me. I ran for dear life to the "Lodge", shoved the papers in the porch and just managed to give one loud bang on the heavy doorknocker before scuttling back to the gates again.

The watchman held them open for me.

"Here, let me do that love, they're much too heavy for you" he said kindly.

I flew back to mother still shivering with fear.

"Don't be silly, he wouldn't hurt you" she said.

It wasn't just him that had scared me, it was all the unknown, unheard of fantasies that, in my mind, surrounded the cemetery.

Much to my delight, we were still able to go to the pictures and, thankfully, there was no queue so we were soon happily settled in our seats laughing at the antics of Laurel and Hardy as Air-Raid Wardens. It quickly took my mind off my earlier mis-haps and fright.

CHAPTER 17

"Make Do and Mend"

17

Mother always dressed my hair in ringlets and I hated having my hair done. It was impossible for me to do my hair myself and, every morning, I had to wait impatiently for her to come in from the shop to attend to my hair. The clock ticked on nearing school time and I became more and more anxious lest I should be late, yet again.

Mother never fully understood why I worried so much about being late for school. She had already explained to my Headmistress that she was single handed in the shop, had the morning papers to see to and a dozen other things as well as getting me ready for school. Aparently, this had not filtered down to my own teacher who was always very annoyed when I, five or ten minutes late, put in an appearance. My own classmates were none too sympathetic either for, as I entered, a loud gasp would go up and that, together with the teachers reprimand, made me want to disappear down the nearest hole in the ground.

I couldn't understand why I could not have plaits or some other simple style that would enable me to cope with it myself. After all, most of the women, including my mother, had changed their hairstyles to fit in with their present mode of living.

The most popular hairstyle at that time was the 'Victory Roll' which consisted of all the hair being tucked into a band of ribbon, shoe lace or elastic band to form a neat roll encircling the whole head. The advantage of this style was that it kept the hair neat and tidy and off the shoulder, essential for safety reasons if you worked in a factory, and within the regulations for those women in the Forces who were not allowed to have their hair touching their shoulders. When 'off duty', the hair could be brushed out and dressed in another popular style such as the Veronica Lake Peek-a-Boo, long and straight with the hair brushed over one eye.

With all the shortages it must have been difficult for the women to still take a pride in their appearance but they did and, once again, ingenuity came to their aid. Silk stockings cost coupons and, as these laddered quickly, they were carefully rolled up, put in the drawer, and kept for 'best'. The remainder of the time the girls painted their legs with leg tan lotion and even got a friend to draw a line up the back of the leg with a dark pencil to simulate the seam in the stocking. When leg lotion was not available, they used gravy powder mixed with water. Fine until they got caught in a shower of rain, then the gravy browning ran down their legs in embarrassing streaks.

Make Do and Mend was essential to ensure our clothes lasted as long as possible. A character called 'Mrs. Sew and Sew'' was featured in the newspapers explaining how last year's dress could be turned into this year's blouse, and an old evening dress turned into a nightdress. Even father's shirt tails did not escape, they made very good aprons she insisted.

Clothing growing children was an extremely difficult problem. The government, recognising the fact that many youngsters were capable of suddenly sprouting up a few inches, rarely wearing their clothes out but rather growing out of them, decided that extra clothing coupons should be allocated. This was, no doubt, the only way of coping with a situation where there was such a variance in size amongst groups of children in the same age bracket. Parents of the larger child had to expend more coupons for their clothes than the parents of a smaller child. It was decided that these extra coupons be allocated to those children above normal size for their age, either by weight, height or foot size.

This meant, of course, that we all had to be regularly weighed and measured at school. Oh, if only the government had realised the agony this was going to mean for those of us who were 'big for our age'.

Our teacher, armed with pen, paper and measuring tape and with scales standing at the ready, set about the task of weighing and measuring her class. As each name was called, we had to walk to the front and stand on the scales whilst she called out our weight to another child who would write it down.

I tried everything possible to stay away from school when I knew it was 'weighing and measuring' day. I was 'big for my age'. "Puppy Fat" mother called it but, to me, it was just plain 'fat' and the humiliation of having to be weighed in front of the class and have the awful truth called out for everyone to hear was almost too much to bear.

I sat at my desk, trying to make myself look very small, in the hope the teacher would overlook me. She never did. When my name was called, I went forward with great trepidation. I tried to stand on the scales on one foot, held my stomach in, stood on the edge but it was no good, and as the teacher revealed the awful truth — why did she have to have such a loud voice, could she not have whispered — the class ooh'd and aaah'd in mock dismay. I went back to my place feeling like Bessie Bunter even though I was by no means the largest in the class.

Of course, it was no better when it came to having our feet measured; mine were larger than they should have been and our teacher refused to measure our feet if our toes were curled up!

Those of us, like myself, who were larger than average then received extra clothing coupons. This, no doubt, delighted our mothers but I'm sure I was not the only one who considered the embarrassment and humiliation hardly worth the few measly extra coupons.

We, ourselves, were not uninventive when it came to making things. Still busy knitting the scarf for my cousin — would it never grow — I began to look enviously at the other girls in our class who had chosen smaller articles to work at like gloves, mittens and helmets. These had now been completed and they were able to move on to the making and embroidering of tablecloths. Of course material was not available for such trifles as tablecloths so they simply went off to the nearest Bakers and purchased a couple of flour bags. Washed, bleached and unpicked they were almost as good as new material.

Whether our teacher felt sorry for me struggling with the scarf or whether she was just as fed up seeing it as I was, I don't know but, quite unexpectedly, she agreed I could start making a tablecloth. I needed no second bidding and soon I was drawing threads around the hem and choosing an embroidery pattern to iron on in each corner. The scarf, I promised faithfully, would be finished at home.

Naturally, when I arrived home from school I always found much more interesting things to do than knitting. How that scarf ever got finished is still a mystery to me.

As Spring gave way to Summer once again, thoughts of holidays began to come to the fore. There was no question of 'going away', it would have to be another 'holiday at home' again this year but now we were getting organised in readiness.

The local Councils began to arrange for many and varied activities to take place in all the local parks. Bands were to play, concerts and exhibitions were to be held.

"Can we go to the park tonight?" I would ask hopefully.

"Why do you want to go there tonight?" my parents asked suspiciously.

"There's a Fair on" I looked from one to the other hopefully.

"We'll see"

176

Oh what an annoying phrase that is. It means neither one thing or another and merely leaves one in an unsatisfactory state of limbo. I waited anxiously for the final decision.

Later, when it had been decided that we would go to the Park, I needed no second telling to get ready. Terry was put on his lead and we were off.

I loved the sideshows at the Fair and the gaudy, rowdy atmosphere, it was so different from anything else. The targets in the shooting range and dart booths all sported caricature pictures of Hitler, Mussolini, Goering and Tojo — the Japanese leader, and we delighted in throwing darts or shooting at these effigies of the men we considered to be evil in the extreme.

Occasionally, side shows that included animals were brought to the Fair. These poor creatures were mainly freaks of nature who had had the misfortune to be born with an extra leg, extra horn or some other disfigurement. "Come and see the only sheep in the world with five legs" the poster said. We did and I felt so sorry for the animals I just wished I could let them loose in the big field. It didn't seem right to me, that they should be shut up like that for the rest of their lives and denied the pleasure of rolling in sweet meadows which was really their birthright.

On Saturday afternoons there were talent competitions. Some contestants were very talented indeed whilst others, quite unintentionally, provided some of the best comedy acts we had seen. The shows were good fun, good value and nearly all played to full capacity audiences.

Still more and more people were being recruited to help with the war effort and, to my horror, not only did the government require human help, they were now looking towards the canine population to assist in the fight against the enemy.

Dogs were now being used on a large scale for guard duties and message carrying and I was very concerned lest Terry should be called up. Mother reassured me that he would not be affected as he was only a small terrier. What was really required were Alsations, Collies, Lurchers and crosses between these breeds as well as Bull Terriers and Bull Mastiffs.

Owners were asked to loan their dogs for service. As it would not have been practical to take all the dogs at the same time, the animal would remain with its owner until 'called up' for special training by the government. Once trained, it then took its place on such special duties as were allocated and, on completion of its war service was returned to its owner and presented with a Certificate of Service. Many of these animals did magnificent service both in the armed forces and in the defence organisations and proved to have courage and tenacity when operating under fire.

August brought a surprise visit from Hitler, when enemy raiders were reported over Merseyside early on the morning of the 10th. It was Merseyside's 500th air-raid since the beginning of the war but involved only a small number of enemy aircraft.

In the wake of this raid we were cheered by the fact that, since the War Savings Campaign began in 1939, the citizens of Liverpool had subscribed to date just under £82,000,000, the highest figure for any City in the country with the exception of London.

There were 1,600 Industrial Savings Groups in Liverpool, 350 Church Groups and an average of one collector to every 100 families in the City. Liverpool was more than doing 'It's bit'.

CHAPTER 18

"Wings for Victory"

18

The long, hazy days of summer were once more giving way to another Autumn and Winter. We did not view the coming of the long nights with as much trepidation as in previous years for the liklihood of air raids was declining more and more.

Suddenly, there was some good news and excitement was rife amongst the adults. 'Allies land at Dieppe!' screamed the massive headlines in the newspapers — could this be the beginning of the long awaited second Front. It was, in fact, a daring commando raid by a military force of Canadians, British Special Service Troops, a small detachment from a U.S. Ranger Battalian together with a small contingent of Fighting French.

It was not the long awaited 'Second Front' that had been so much talked about, but an audacious experiment carried out with precision and bravado. Its mission was the laying down of a pattern for future landings when, it was hoped, a permanent bridgehead would be established and the way opened for the great march of liberation across Europe.

We certainly needed some good news for, although we may have won the Battle of Britain, things were not going well in other areas. Rommel was advancing in the Desert and was well on his way into Egypt.

At home, the work of repairing our ravaged homes had begun and, during the latter part of 1942 new houses began springing up on the bomb sites as part of a corporation scheme to provide 158 houses, not only for air-raid victims, but to give the City a good start in the post-war housing scheme. These new houses were originally known as half-houses and were followed later by others of a somewhat similar design and called Pre-fabs.

November arrived and we had something to celebrate at last. The tide had turned in the Desert warfare and the 8th Army was advancing swiftly. Rommel was being chased back and the Italians, who were also fighting in the Desert, were being rounded up in their thousands as prisoners. We were delighted by the newsreels at the cinema showing columns and columns of Italian prisoners being marched away to the Prisoner of War camps with just a couple of British soldiers on guard. It was truly the beginning of the end for Hitler and Mussolini we felt.

Buoyed up by the good news from the Front, we began to look forward again. Christmas was coming and we were going to win. Although Father Christmas had to put a notice in the local paper to say that unfortunately, due to the paper shortage he would not be able to answer his letters this year, the children carried on writing. The Liverpool "Echo" put everyones feelings in a nutshell when they wished all their readers "A Brighter Christmas".

After the holiday itself, we had the pantomime season to look forward to and we went to the Empire to see Jack Buchanan in 'Cinderella'. The Royal Court were staging 'The Maid of the Mountains' whilst the Pavilion stayed traditional with 'Red Riding Hood' featuring Jack Daly and Jimmy Clitheroe. Things were certainly looking brighter and the New Year came in, peaceful and without incident, save for the usual spate of coughs and colds.

Those of us who, like myself, were barely seven years old when the war started had now spent quite a deal of our formative years in a wartime atmosphere and many younger children knew no other way of life. Up to the age of five, a child's world consists only of its own home and family, near relations and the close vicinity of home and friends who live nearby. School is the first major step into the outside world and the realisation that there are other powers of authority beyond parents and very close relatives.

For those in my age group, schooling had barely begun before the world was plunged into one of the worst conflicts history had ever known. Naturally our whole world and the learning about it was coloured by the momentous events taking place in our lifetime. Unlike the adults we, sadly, began to accept it as normal.

Family life was completely disrupted as the menfolk were either away fighting in the Desert, the jungles of the Far East or sailing the high seas defending our coastlines and bringing in the much needed supplies. Children born just prior to and during the early years of the war often grew up without knowing their fathers. All they had was a photograph, brought out regularly by Mummy, who pointed to the strange man and told them he was 'Daddy'.

One such child who lived near to us caused great consternation in the family when his father arrived home on 'leave'. Used to going out alone with his mother he kept looking at his father and pointedly enquired 'Do we have to take him with us everywhere we go mummy?'

Now, we could safely go to the pictures without the fear of air-raids. No more the sudden announcement that the sirens were sounding, the guns were firing, we could watch the film in peace. We flocked there in our thousands for it was a great form of escapism. It also brought home to us how different our way of life was to that portrayed on the screen.

The beautiful, lavishly furnished houses of Hollywood with their vast rooms and luxurious swimming pools seemed to be a world away from us. Here, it was now impossible to buy anything other than second-hand furniture or 'Utility' and that only with a permit.

Sometimes we would see films set in far distant countries such as Arabia, where handsome Sheiks and glamorous girls sat around large swimming pools basking in the sun whilst servants brought in large baskets of fruit. Rosy red apples, luscious oranges, bananas, pineapples, grapes and other mouthwatering delicacies were theirs for the asking. As soon as these appeared on the screen the audience would sigh loud ooh's and aah's, for it had been many years since we had been privileged to taste such luxuries. In fact, when bananas eventually came into the country, many children had to be taught how to eat them.

Occasionally, however, the editors of the newsreels gave us a good laugh. Sometimes these were even better than the comedy films, for they cleverly altered and edited film of Hitler and his cronies to make it appear as if they were doing silly walks and dancing 'The Lambeth Walk' whilst marching along. The whole cinema would rock with laughter at these strange antics.

It was fun to see Hitler and his cronies doing strange things. We were all involved in this dreadful conflict and everyone's way of life had changed.

The gypsy population, often maligned and treated as second class citizens, came into their own. There were about 45,000 genuine Romanies in this country and they were only too willing to help, offering their own particular Romany skills.

Romany girls with fingers supple from weaving baskets, became expert at wiring electrical equipment and other complicated work. Those used to making poachers nets, constructed nets large enough to cover and sling cargoes or use as camouflage, both on land and at sea.

Many Romanies were honoured for their work in the Civil Defence. Their service was invaluable in rescue work for their eyes were trained to darkness and they were able to find their way through a tangled maze of wreckage at night. Romanies were also found in every branch of HM Forces, including the women's branches. One

182

Romany lad, a hero of the air, went to the Palace to receive his medal from the King but, sadly, later died in action.

During the early part of the year, it was announced that there was to be another huge drive in the War Savings Campaign. This time it was to be "Wings for Victory Week" and the City put in a wholehearted effort to make this an unprecedented success.

On Saturday, 8th May, parades and demonstrations took place all over Liverpool. In the City Centre, a Parade of the Services and Merchant Navies of the Allied Nations took place in Lime Street whilst on St. George's Plateau, the RAF Central Band took their place to entertain the crowds viewing the Air Rescue Launch and Banks Crusader Tanks. The Royal Marines Band played at the Wings for Victory Pavilion in Church Street whilst at the Tunnel Entrance there was an exhibition of Balloon Barrage Drill.

As all these celebrations were taking place in Town, we were in Walton Hall Park, excitedly awaiting the arrival of the "Wings for Victory Week" queen who was to be crowned on the Bandstand. For once the weather was kind and the sun shone down as the queen and her entourage arrived, smiling and waving, to the crowds. After the crowning there were to be demonstrations and contests between men and women firefighters.

As I already ran a Savings Group, I planned to collect as much as I possibly could during this week and, to this end, I set up a display on the far side of the counter in our shop. The centrepiece of my display was Terry, dressed up in a pair of red, white and blue crepe paper wings.

"He'll never sit there like that" said my parents.

But he did.

Taking a break every now and again to stretch his legs, Terry sat patiently beside me most of that week and we did a roaring trade in Savings Stamps and Certificates.

The Parades and exhibitions continued all week and, on the Tuesday, the exciting news came through that one citizen alone, who wished to remain anonymous, had donated £40,000 to buy outright the Halifax bomber on display in Church Street. It was now to bear the name "City of Liverpool".

The target of £11,000,000 had now been passed and we began aiming for an extra million a day till Saturday to achieve a new target of £15,000,000. This was passed by noon on the Friday and there was still a day and a half to go. When the final count was made, all records to date outside London had been broken. The Lord Mayor announced a massive figure of £16,799,069 had been reached.

As a celebration, our teacher decided to take the whole class to New Brighton for a day out. This, in itself, was something of an occasion for we sailed on the "Royal Daffodil II" which had been sunk off Seacombe Landing Stage during the May 1941 Blitz and had now been successfully refloated and put back into service.

We had a glorious day on the beach. The sun shone out of a brilliant blue sky as we played around the rock pools by the old lighthouse. At mid-day we were all assembled by the boating lake to eat our sandwiches and plan the afternoon's activities which was to include a game of cricket.

Once the teams were chosen and the match begun, the shore was soon echoing to our excited screams and shouts as we chased backwards and forwards after the ball. One particular young lad displayed great prowess at batting and sent the ball right up the side of the boating lake. A lone soldier, walking near at the time, retrieved the ball and stopped to watch the game. On several occasions he joined in by running for the ball and, in doing so, managed to strike up a conversation with our teacher. Naturally, this led to much winking and giggling on our part.

Sometime later, as we lay on the hot sand sipping lemonade, exhausted from our activity, one of the boys let out a low whistle.

"Hey, look over there" he crowed.

We looked.

Our teacher, comfortably settled in a rowing boat, was being happily rowed around the lake by the soldier.

Thirty eager little heads shot up to watch their progress, all thoughts of resting forgotten.

"Do you think he's trying to get off with her?"

"Nar, don't be soft."

"Wonder if she'll bring him back with us?"

By the time our teacher arrived back to join us we had got the two of them well and truly married off. No doubt she must have felt a little embarrassed for there were more than a few winks and nudges. The soldier did not come back with us.

On September 3rd, 1943, exactly four years after the start of the war, Italy was invaded by British and Canadian troops. The Russian forces were driving nearer and nearer to the Ukraine capital and Hitler was in the process of being defeated on all fronts.

We felt the first chill winds of autumn with hearts warm with hope, our spirits lifted by the news from the Front. When the news came on the wireless it seemed to cheer everyone up and even I was interested enough to enquire what was happening.

"The war's nearly over, it won't be long now" was the satisfying answer.

Christmas came around once more. People saved their coupons for just such a time and it was probably the one time in the year when we sold more than a quarter of sweets at a time to the same customer. The adults were better at saving sweet coupons than the children, who mostly spent their ration within the first week of the four week period, and just hoped their parents would take pity on them and share their own later. They invariably did.

The week prior to Christmas, mother was busy serving a strange lady. She had about four ration books full of sweet coupons to spend and mother weighed and bagged each quarter as the lady made her selection, obviously stocking up for Christmas.

Whilst this was proceeding, young Jimmy Evans came in with his mother and they took their place by the counter waiting to be served. Jimmy was only four years old and a lovable little rascal with dark curly hair and twinkling brown eyes. Those same dark eyes began to grow as wide as saucers as he watched bag after bag of sweets piling up on the counter. Suddenly, unable to contain himself any longer he turned to his mother.

"She's a greedy bugger isn't she Mum, there'll be none left for us."

Mother had to bend down under the counter whilst she stifled her laughter in a fit of coughing. I disappeared quickly into the living room convulsed.

Poor Jimmy, he had never before in his life seen so many bags of sweets going to one person.

The expression on the lady's face had to be seen to be believed. She turned to see who had made the remark and was just in time to see Jimmy being bustled out of the shop by his very red faced mother.

CHAPTER 19

"The Invasion"

19

The coming of 1944 heralded real hope that the tide had now turned in our favour and it would not be too long before our fight against Hitler would be over.

A small, insect-type, character called the 'Squander Bug' began cropping up everywhere. It was featured on the posters pasted up on the hoardings covering the old bomb sites. It appeared in newspapers and at the Cinema and we were continually being told not to listen to it when it whispered in your ear such things as "Ask for more wages", "Buy lots of things you don't need", "waste fuel", "Use as much as you want".

The idea behind this was to make everyone stop and think twice before buying or using anything that was not absolutely essential. "The squander bug will get you if you won't watch out" became a popular catchphrase.

This need to save and the dreadful shortages were causing our mothers quite a headache, for our school was engaged in the exciting prospect of putting on a pantomime of our very own and much was needed in the way of costumes, props and scenery.

Miss Sharpe, our Headmistress, had booked Crane Theatre in Hanover Street, the auditions had taken place and we were all very busy learning parts and rehearsing for the big event.

The pantomime was to be the classic "Cinderella" and the leading role went to a girl in my own class who possessed a very beautiful singing voice and some considerable talent as a ballerina.

Each day a little time was set aside for rehearsals, the principals often staying behind after school to rehearse their own individual parts. Friday afternoons at Swainsons were completely put over to rehearsals. We were all totally behind this seemingly ambitious endeavour and determined to make every effort to ensure its success.

Costumes were planned and, whilst arrangements were made to have these made up by a dressmaker, it was the mothers who had to provide the necessary clothing coupons for the material. Wigs were required, especially for the ballroom scene. What a headache they turned out to be as mothers pondered on how to set about making them. Some managed very well with cotton wool whilst others obtained a fine white wool from local hairdressers, usually used for winding round the ends of the hair during the perming process.

Excitement mounted as we watched the days tick away on the calendar and, all too soon it seemed, Miss Sharpe was asking us to try and sell as many tickets as possible.

Eventually the big night arrived and we met at the Theatre, well scrubbed, our hair shining from recent shampooing and our eyes aglow with excitement. We were shown into our respective dressing rooms, helped into our costumes and then, the best part of all, wrapped in a large towel whilst the make-up was applied. We eyed the big boxes of real stage greasepaint with wonder — oh to be set loose with that lot.

Soon we could hear noises coming from the auditorium and we knew the audience were beginning to take their places. The orchestra filed in, the first notes of the introduction were struck and a loud voice shouted "Everyone in the opening chorus to the wings, quickly now". Our pantomime had begun.

In between scenes, we rushed back to our dressing rooms and, after one quick change, discovered someone had left the big box of greasepaint on the table. The temptation was too great.

"I think I need a bit more lipstick."

"I need some more eyeshadow."

"Can I borrow the lipstick after you?"

We painted our faces and admired ourselves in the mirror until one of the teachers came in. The greasepaint was quickly removed out of reach and then, much to our disgust, the teacher proceeded to clean our faces leaving us with even less make-up than when we'd begun.

The show went on and the audience showed their appreciation with much clapping of hands. The fairies dance was meant to be pretty and simplistic with the tiniest members of the school performing a simple routine involving a few easy steps and much raising and lowering of wings which were attached to their skirts and little fingers. The tiniest member of the fairy band was about three to four years old and stood beside her elder sister. Each time the little one raised her wings she discovered she was showing her knickers. Hastily she tried to pull down her skirt but each time she lifted her wings the white frilly knickers were once again on display. Her attempts at trying to cover her knickers soon came to the attention of her sister who began nudging and whispering to her. The audience were entranced and dissolved into helpless laughter at the antics of the two small fairies. Backstage, we could hear the laughter and wondered what on earth was going on. There was a sudden rush to find peepholes in the curtains and soon, we too were rocking with mirth just like the audience.

Eventually the show was over and we all trooped on stage for the Finale. Bouquets were presented to Miss Sharpe and the other helpers, thanks were offered to all concerned, not least our mothers, and then the orchestra struck up with "God Save The King" and the audience rose to its feet to join in the National Anthem. The final curtain came down and it was time to go home and leave the magic behind.

We soon changed into our outdoor clothes but were very reluctant to remove our make-up. As a special treat we were allowed to leave it on until we got home. What a magical start to a year that was to be full of excitement.

Rumours of a forthcoming invasion were now rife and our forces, together with all the impedimenta of an invasion force began massing in the South of England. There were so many people, and so much equipment, all in one place at one point that a joke started going around that England was top heavy and would soon tip over into the Channel.

On the morning of June 6th, 1944, the long awaited reports started to come through. The Invasion of France had begun. Under the command of General Eisenhower, Allied Naval Forces, supported by strong air forces, began landing Allied armies on the northern coast of France. Over 4,000 ships and thousands of other craft had made up an Armada which had crossed the Channel. Massed airborne landings had been successfully effected behind the enemy's lines and the Commanders who were engaged reported that everything was going according to plan.

The excitement was intense, the newspaper headlines were the biggest I had ever seen. The news was listened to avidly and everywhere people were talking about the Invasion.

My mother was very worried about my cousin in the Royal Navy. We did not know for sure where he was, due to the censorship, but mother had a strong feeling he might have been involved in the Invasion. This feeling was strengthened when, one morning, she awoke in some distress to tell us that she had had a dream in which she heard knocking on our front door. Opening the door she had found my cousin standing on the doorstep, swathed in bandages. Nothing could persuade her that something hadn't happened to him.

Two days later, there was a knock on our front door. My cousin's wife had come to tell us his ship had been mined and he was in hospital in Normandy. Thankfully, my cousin and most of his shipmates were safe but the ship and all their possessions had been lost. Two month's earlier, I had at last managed to finish that wretched scarf and, after the final fringe had been sewn on, I carefully pressed and packed it off in the post. Now, thanks to Hitler, it was deep down on a seabed in the English Channel.

Even at this late stage in the war, it seemed that evacuation was to once again rear its ugly head. This time, however, it was not the children of Liverpool who were to go away but rather we were to be hosts to the children of London and the South. Hitler, in a last ditch effort to regain some credibility had produced the most dastardly weapon so far — a flying bomb. Attacks on the South of England began on 15th June and, without any warning, these dreadful weapons fell to the ground exploding with results equivalent to 1,000 kilogramme bombs.

Trainloads of evacuees arrived at Birkenhead. Four hundred went to Heswall. Hoylake promised to accommodate eight hundred distributed amongst West Kirby, Greasby and Meols. On July 20th, it was announced that since 2nd July, over 170,000 women and children had been evacuated from London to other parts of the country whilst another 3,000 were due to go later in the month.

At the end of July, we broke up from school and, for me, it was my last term at Spellow Lane for it had now been decided that I should attend St. Edmund's Grammar School for Girls in Princes Park. For the first time in my life I was to wear school uniform and it was with much excitement that I accompanied my mother to George Henry Lees, the big department store in Town, to purchase a new gymslip, tie, blouses and all the other necessary items.

"Make the most of the summer holidays for there'll be some hard work ahead of you" was mother's advice.

As it happened, August Bank Holiday proved to be the best Bank Holiday of the War, for it was now possible to move more freely into the country and the seaside. The main drift, for people in Liverpool, was towards the Pier Head for a day out at New Brighton, West Kirby and the other beauty spots on the Wirral whilst many headed the opposite way towards Southport, Formby and even as far as Blackpool.

By September, Paris was free for the first time since its occupation in June 1940 and the battle was now on German soil with powerful tank forces thrusting into the Reich whilst the British Second Army pushed into Holland and the Russians marched forward in the Baltic.

As the Allied forces pressed forward they were now able to set free many Prisoner of War camps and the men who had been imprisoned there for so long were finally repatriated back to their homelands. Whenever it was known that a local man was coming home, the neighbours went wild with joy. Red, white and blue bunting was hung from window to window decorating the whole of the street in which he lived. Union Jacks were hung out of windows and large signs strung across the width of the road with the words "WELCOME HOME BILLY — 3 YEARS A POW". On the day of the actual homecoming, the whole neighbourhood would be there to welcome him as he turned into the road carrying his heavy kitbag. Huge celebrations followed, often lasting late into the night.

Amidst all this joyous news from Europe, bitter battles were still going on against the Japanese in the Pacific War Zone and it was with great joy that news was received of landings, on an even bigger scale than those in Normandy, that had taken place on the Island of Leyte splitting the Japanese force in half in the Phillipines.

Not even the first snow of winter, which fell in Derbyshire in early November, could dampen our spirits as we prepared for the best Christmas we had had for many years. Father Christmas was waiting in the Toy Fair department at the Bon Marche with an assortment of jungle animals to guard the entrance to his magic cave whilst our armies guarded the entrance to Germany. The final stages of the war in Europe were about to begin.

The pantomime "Cinderella"

192

CHAPTER 20

"Victory At Last"

20

December, 1944 proved to be the coldest since 1939 and, as January dawned with temperatures still below freezing, housewives became more and more concerned as to how they were going to provide a hot meal. We were now suffering from one of the worst potato shortages ever known.

The position was getting desperate as long queues formed up outside the greengrocers. Some took to employing a rather dubious form of trading by refusing to serve potatoes unless other goods were purchased as well. Others initiated their own form of rationing and allowed each customer two or three pounds regardless of whether other goods were purchased. Even these meagre supplies were soon exhausted and then there were no potatoes to be had at any price.

As soon as a delivery van was spotted word went round quickly and the queues started forming. The women stood for hours and the local wags soon got busy. Where, only recently, large signs had welcomed home the men returning from the Prisoner of War Camps, others now appeared. Similar in every way, they read "WELCOME HOME MAGGIE, 3 HOURS IN THE POTATO QUEUE".

The weather remained bitterly cold with temperatures well below freezing. To our joy we discovered Walton Hall Park lake had frozen over. Dare we try and slide on it. Gingerly I tested its strength with a tentative foot.

"It's alright, it's quite safe, you can go on it if you want" a deep voice boomed in my ear. It was the old Park Keeper.

Go on it. I nearly skidded to the opposite side in fright for I hadn't heard him coming up behind me.

"It's been a pretty hard frost so the ice is quite thick. Anyway they were skating on it last night. If it can hold them I daresay it'll hold you lot." For once he was smiling. Usually he spent his time scowling and shouting "Get off those trees", "Get away from that lake", "Don't you start picking those flowers" whilst we, with a quick warning shout "It's the Parky", scattered as quickly as we could.

We needed no second bidding and were soon enjoying ourselves sliding on the ice. When I arrived home I was soaking wet from falling and sliding on the ice and snow.

"Go and get those wet things off and change into something dry before you get your death of cold", I was told.

Still boiling hot from all the sliding and running I dug out an old summer dress to put on.

"For goodness sake use your commonsense" mother told me as I was sent back once again to change. I thought I had done.

We were now getting more and more indications that the war was nearly over in Europe. Oranges arrived in this country from Spain and an allocation of one pound per ration book for the period 15th to 19th January, was made. The men were continuing to return home from the Middle East and the Prisoner of War Camps. In Europe itself, the Allies were fast closing in on Berlin.

At home, the abolition of the blackout was planned for April. Unfortunately, however, Merseyside was to be excluded from this relaxation of the regulations, for enemy submarines were still on the prowl in the Irish Sea and it was considered too much of a risk for Liverpool to turn the lights back on.

For some reason it now became almost impossible to purchase a pair of shoes. We had the necessary coupons but stocks had become sadly depleted and the range of styles and sizes on offer in the shops were nearly always unsuitable. After several expeditions into Town in search of a pair of shoes for me we returned home, yet again, empty handed. I was secretly very pleased about this for I did not want an ordinary pair of shoes, I wanted a pair of "Woodies".

"Woodies" were wooden soled shoes, a new fashion in footwear, introduced to alleviate the problem. In no way did these "woodies" resemble the old 'clogs' worn years ago in the Lancashire Cotton Mills. Our "woodies' were fashioned in a variety of styles and the uppers were made of leather or suede. The soles were often hinged in two places to make for ease of walking. Several of my friends already had them and I was delighted when I too was allowed them. Mother had been most reluctant to buy them for she thought they were far too heavy and would be bad for the feet. Now, with the shortage of shoes, there was really no choice.

We were now eagerly awaiting the capitulation of Germany and there was much talk of Surrender Terms being considered by the German High Command. Mussolini had been captured and we saw macabre pictures of him hanging upside down in the street whilst the local populace pelted his body with rotten vegetables.

There was little hope now for Hitler and the Nazis but they still held out and refused to surrender to the Allies, particularly to Russia. It was thought they were fearful of the retribution that might come their way for the dreadful deeds perpetrated against the Russians

195

during the siege of Leningrad and, indeed, they certainly had cause to be fearful for they had done some dreadful things to the people of that City.

Retribution was indeed to come, and the strongest feelings against the Nazis were aroused when the horrific details of their Concentration Camps at Dachau, Belson and Buchenwald were revealed to the world. When the Allies entered these barbaric death camps no-one was left in any doubt that this was one war that had had to be fought and won.

I couldn't bear to watch the terrible scenes portrayed on the newsreels and hid my face until they were over. In Dachau alone, 32,000 prisoners were liberated, 9,000 died of hunger and disease whilst 4,000 had perished in the cold winter months. Belson and Buchenwald all told their own stories of the evil inhumane treatment that had been metered out to innocent victims not prepared to go along with Hitler's regime.

On Monday, 7th May, 1945 it was announced that Germany had surrendered unconditionally to all the Allies including the Russians. The following day Mr. Churchill announced the end of the war in Europe and later that night King George VI spoke to the Empire. It was VE Day. There was peace in Europe at last. Oh how we celebrated.

The whole country went wild with joy. Various Royal Navy Commands in Liverpool held a special service in the Open Air at the Pier Head. Bonfires were lit all over the City. Red, white and blue flew triumphantly from every window.

My father got out a large Union Jack and hung it on a big flag pole from the bedroom window. The whole of City Road was a mass of flags and bunting, as were all the side streets. Street parties were planned and I ran off to Dyson Street where arrangements for our party were already well in hand. The mothers got together and pooled resources. Each family contributed towards a 'kitty' and from this all the food was provided.

"Don't forget you've got to wear red, white and blue tonight", I was reminded as I ran back home, full of excitement, to tell my parents about the party.

Father made me a red, white and blue hat from some old crepe paper and, later that afternoon we were thoroughly enjoying the celebrations. Long tables, covered in red, white and blue, were laid out down the centre of the street and the food carefully placed on it. Everyone lent chairs, crockery and cutlery and a huge bonfire was laid ready; this would be set alight later in the evening. We made a huge effigy of Hitler and this was put on top of the bonfire.

The mothers hovered at the back as we took our places at the table and the party commenced. The noise was terrific as we all talked and laughed between mouthfuls of sandwiches and cake. Soon it was time to clear away the tables and the menfolk made short work of that. We played games and enjoyed the competitions and races that the adults had arranged. As darkness began to fall the huge bonfire was lit to rousing cheers and we all formed a huge circle and danced around it. Large potatoes were thrust into the glowing embers to roast until their skins were crisp and black, the centres soft and fluffy. An old gramophone was brought out so that the adults could dance and we joined in as best we could.

All good things have to come to an end and, as the excitement of this wonderful celebration began to take its toll, most of us found it hard to keep our eyes open.

Every City celebrated that night. In the centre of Liverpool, the crowds massed around the Town Hall and danced in the streets whilst, over the water in Birkenhead, Hamilton Square became the centre point for the celebrations. Bebington's Mayer Hall was decorated with red, white and blue bunting and fairy lights and floodlights lit the park. Wallasey, Hoylake, Bootle and Crosby all told the same story whilst Lord Street, Southport looked like a veritable fairyland. The bells of Chester Cathedral rang out and Services of Thanksgiving were held in the great Cathedral.

Huge Victory Parades were planned and the Sunday after VE Day, we all went to St. Georges Plateau to watch the Lord Mayor take the Salute as representatives of every war time service paraded before him to the accompaniment of massed bands.

The celebrations over, it was back to reality again. The war in the Pacific was still waging against the Japanese and many of our men were still engaged in bitter battle, others were held in the dreadful Prisoner of War Camps.

Meanwhile, the government in this country had decided to hold an Election, the first since the war began. I couldn't remember what a General Election was like and thought it very exciting.

We discussed the candidates between ourselves and, not knowing anything about politics, decided to support the youngest and, in our opinion, best looking candidate.

"You have to consider what's best for the country" my father tried to explain.

197

Many people were surprised as the Labour Party swept into power. It had seemed as if Winston Churchill's own personal popularity and great leadership in bringing us safely through the war in Europe would alone have been sufficient to secure an overwhelming victory for the Conservatives. The public, however, obviously had other ideas.

America also, by now, had a new Leader for, sadly, President Roosevelt had died just before the final announcement of the capitulation of Germany. Their new leader Harry Truman met with the Leaders of all the Allied Countries and, together, they took one of the most momentous decisions of the war. In order to save as many lives as possible and finish the war in the quickest possible time, the Atomic Bomb was to be dropped on Japan.

The news of this new and horrific weapon being dropped on Hiroshima on 6th August, 1945 stunned the world. Never had one bomb caused so much devastation. Pictures in the newspapers showed miles and miles of desolation. Radioactive rays had spread, killing and wounding those who had not actually died in the searing heat of the initial explosion.

A second Atomic Bomb was dropped on 9th August, this time on the town of Nagasaki and Russia declared war on Japan. With this new and dreadful weapon, there was nothing the Japanese could do but surrender unconditionally. On Friday, 10th August, 1945 it was all over, Japan was ready to surrender. The war in the Pacific was over. The world was at peace again.

Once again we set about celebrating the Victory with more joyous celebrations. Another street party, more dancing in the streets. Flags and bunting flying from every building and Victory Parades in every Town and City thoughout the country.

In London, the opening of the new Parliament on 15th August, 1945 marked VJ Day and the Royal Procession became a Victory drive with people lining the route, cheering and waving their flags at the Royal Family.

At long last the struggle was over, the battle was won. We were victorious but the world had inherited the worst, and most fearful, weapon it had ever known — the Atomic Bomb.

Had this weapon been invented all those years ago when I, as a small child of six years old, stood at the kitchen table asking my mother "What's a war like Mummy?" my childhood might have been a different story. I, and many others, might not have had a story to tell, it could all have been over in a matter of minutes or, it may never have happened at all.

We had bad times. We went short of many things. We were often frightened and fearful, especially during the blitz. We laughed, we cried. We had happy times as well during those terrible years but, most important of all, we survived. May we continue to win the Peace and may future generations of children never find out "What a war is really like".

THE END

The pantomime "Cinderella".

OTHER TITLES FROM

Countyvise

Local History

Birkenhead Priory	Jean McInniss
Birkenhead Park	Jean McInniss
The Spire is Rising	Dorothy Harden
Neston and Parkgate	Jeffrey Pearson
Scotland Road	Terry Cooke
Helen Forrester Walk	K. Rickard
Women at War	Pat Ayres
Merseyside Moggies	R.M. Lewis
Dream Palaces	Harold Ackroyd
Forgotten Shores	Maurice Hope
Storm over the Mersey	Beryl Wade
Memories of Heswall 1935 — 1985	Heswall W.E.A.
Poverty Deserved?	Pat Ayres
Chinese Liverpudlians	Maria Wong

Local Railway Titles

Seventeen Stations to Dingle	John W. Gahan
The Line Beneath the Liners	John W. Gahan
Steel Wheels to Deeside	John W. Gahan
Seaport to Seaside	John W. Gahan
A Portrait of Wirral's Railways	Roger Jermy

Local Shipping Titles

Sail on the Mersey	Michael Stammers
Ghost Ships on the Mersey	K.J. Williams
The Liners of Liverpool – *Part I*	Derek Whale
The Liners of Liverpool – *Part II*	Derek Whale
The Liners of Liverpool – *Part III*	Derek Whale
Hands off the Titanic	Monica O'Hara
Mr. Merch and other stories	Ken Smith

Local Sport

The Liverpool Competition (Local Cricket)	P.N. Walker
Lottie Dod	Jeffrey Pearson

History with Humour

The One-Eyed City	Rod Mackay
Hard Knocks	Rod Mackay
The Binmen are coming	Louis Graham

Natural History

Birdwatching in Cheshire	Eric Hardy

Other Titles

Speak through the Earthquake, Wind & Fire	Graham A. Fisher
It's Me, O Lord	Members of Heswall Churches
Companion to the Fylde	R.K. Davies
Country Walks on Merseyside – *Part I*	David Parry
Country Walks on Merseyside – *Part II*	David Parry
A-Z Cheshire Ghosts	Muriel Armand
The Courtship of Knocker Yates	Robert Brown